THE LAW OF FAITH

THE LAW OF FAITH

by

NORMAN P. GRUBB

CHRISTIAN LITERATURE CRUSADE
FORT WASHINGTON   PENNSYLVANIA

CHRISTIAN LITERATURE CRUSADE
Fort Washington, Pennsylvania 19034

CANADA
Box 189, Elgin, Ontario   KOG 1EO

GREAT BRITAIN
The Dean, Alresford, Hampshire

AUSTRALIA
P. O. Box 91, Pennant Hills, N.S.W. 2120

NEW ZEALAND
Box 1688, Auckland, C.1

First published 1947
Paperback edition 1970

ISBN 0-87508-223-8

Printed in U.S.A.

CONTENTS

CONTENTS

In 1940 a little book was published called *Touching the Invisible*. A promise was then made of another book to follow, which would deal more fully with the spiritual truths touched upon in its pages. This book is the promised attempt.

It has not been lightly written; indeed, after practically completing the manuscript some four years ago, it has now again been almost entirely rewritten.

The truths contained in it have been central to my life for many years. In putting them on paper, I feel that I am passing on to others the most precious and innermost secrets that God has taught me, and I have long felt that I could never rest satisfied till I had committed them to writing. Of recent years, too, perhaps through many attempts to expound them, some points that were more obscure to me have become much clearer, and I have felt more able to give an outline of them.

At the same time, I keenly realize the truth of Paul's saying: "If any man think that he knoweth everything, he knoweth nothing yet as he ought to know." I realize how careful we have to be to see that any "view of truth" we have is really and truly "the truth as it is in Jesus"; also that any viewpoint we may hold is only one "find" from that all-embracing treasury of wisdom and knowledge which is "hid in Christ". Others come back from their search with jewels equally or much more precious. If there is a thesis of truth, there is also an antithesis, and the balance of the Word of God is to be sought and maintained.

In that spirit, therefore, of readiness to be shown where we may err in emphasis, and of appreciation of complementary and counterbalancing aspects of truth, I hope that God may bless these chapters and make them of as practical benefit in the daily life as I have found them to be.

My thanks are due to many: to my wife who has drunk at the same fountains with me these twenty-five years and been a constant source of encouragement; to the many, past and present, well known and less known, from whose writings light has poured into my soul; to those who have given freely of their love and labour in typing and preparing the manuscript, especially to my constant co-worker, Fred W. Anthony, and to Miss Muriel Geer and Mrs. Pluckrose (then Miss Alice Clark); to James S. Finlay, whose careful reading and forthright criticisms helped me to adjust many things: to the Revs. Jack Ford and Noel Brooks, whose expert opinions on various aspects of chapter 12, in which they are specialists, were of great help; to Jock Purves for several illuminating suggestions; and finally to William and Ena Pethybridge, who have carefully checked the manuscript and made many helpful alterations.

NORMAN P. GRUBB

Norwood,
   January 1946

Chapter One

THE life of faith has had a fascination for me for over twenty-five years. So far as I remember, this interest was first quickened through the study of George Müller's life; then by the fact of a clear call from God to join a "faith" mission, which was at that time best known by its earlier name of Heart of Africa Mission, but is now known by its enlarged, though clumsier, title of Worldwide Evangelization Crusade. Obedience to this call meant that fascinating theory must now be translated into action. Straight away the challenge came from the one who had toiled and sacrificed to give me a good start in life: Would I not be wiser to join some society, enter some denomination, which, if ill-health invalided me from the mission field, I might find some guaranteed sphere of ministry and livelihood at home?

But the call had been so clear that adherence to it was not difficult, except for the momentary pain it caused to loved ones, and that was not of long duration, for when they saw that the decision was definite, they gladly and warmly commended me to the will of God.

Twelve years passed, spent partly in the Belgian Congo, partly on journeyings oft as emissary from field to home-end on mission matters, and partly in translation work. Not much opportunity was afforded for the practice of faith in any specialized sense, or rather it may be more correct to say that the secret of the application of Scriptural and achieving faith had not yet been seen, and therefore the many opportunities for applying it were not perceived. Personal needs were regularly supplied, mainly through the channel of the mission; and, as I have just said, the meaning and use of faith as God's instrument of deliverance in all the other problems of life, internal and external, had not yet dawned upon me. The pull of faith, however, its attraction and fascination, never left me. It had become a deep inner conviction. I had glimpsed and tasted. It is my belief that in each member of Christ's body, from the time of the new birth, the Holy Spirit begins to develop some special characteristic through which God may be glorified in a particular way, some aspect of His grace and truth through which the whole body may be edified and enlightened. Such are the gifts of the Spirit, about which more will be said later: and in one's own case I humbly believe that it was God who maintained in one this special thirst and attraction for the way of faith, this readiness to absorb all light concerning it, and to venture one's life in the excercise of it. Real opportunities were bound to come, as well as real enlightenment, at the right moment, and that moment was when I was ready to see and take them; for the real fact was that those intervening years had first to be spent in internal adjustments: the secrets of faith had to be discovered and applied in the solution of one's own inner problems, in the satisfaction of one's own soul-thirst, in the snapping of the chain of one's own self-centredness, in the transference of oppressing heart burdens to the One who had given Himself to bear them. These experiences also will be woven later into our whole examination of the texture of faith, for that aspect of the life of faith is antecedent to all others. A faith that works first in our own lives can then, and only then, be applied to the problems around us.

There is a school of faith, and there is a life of faith. At school we are private individuals: we learn, we experiment, we try things out by ourselves and on ourselves, we gradually grasp a technique. In life we take responsibility, we are in the public eye; other lives depend on us; we are supposed to know our job and apply our knowledge; the wheels of our particular industry are kept going by us. My years in the school of faith lasted till 1931, my thirteenth year as a missionary. As I now look back, I can see quite clearly when the transition took place in my experience; the school was left (although in another sense we are very much permanent pupils), the life of faith begun. With the key to my inner problems in my hands through the grace of God and illumination of the Spirit, a clearcut position of faith was taken in a certain matter, under pressure of the Spirit, involving my wife and myself to our financial limit. There is no need to go into details which were comparatively trivial. The duration of the rest was six months. The day of crisis came in the middle when I almost succumbed and was only saved by walking to the post office and sending off a letter which once again staked everything on God's faithfulness. The deliverance actually began to come to me within ten minutes, on the pavement outside that post office, starting with a trickle and rising to a flood. It was all very mundane but to me it was a landmark. Schooldays were nearing their end. The master key which could open a very little material door could just as easily be applied to great gateways of world-wide opportunity in the Kingdom of God.

Then followed three years of great illumination in the way of faith. It was as if that which had been seen dimly as a series of separate peaks of faith which might occasionally, with much effort, be scaled, was now seen to be a broad high road in the uplands, a route of the Spirit, a way of life to be steadily traversed, and no range of rugged peaks at all. The Scriptures were marvellously opened up: Hebrews 11 especially became alive, and faith was seen to be the permanent element in which the men of God lived, men who themselves had first to pass through the school into the life of faith—Abraham, Jacob, Moses, Joshua, Gideon, David, and so through all the list into New Testament days. They were days of great revelation; it was like the thrill of a new discovery, the exaltation of the explorer whose eyes are resting for the first time in history on some magnificent landscape. Experiments were made, feebly made, but the feet were not firm enough yet on their new road to take one to the destination, and nothing came of it. But the light had truly dawned, Scriptural light, borne witness to by the inner assurance of the Spirit, the consummation without doubt of the gropings and inner preparations of years. Failures could not quench those certainties. All that was needed was a firmer grasp of method, and, above all, those special sorts of circumstances in which living faith through all history has thrived, those necessary conditions for its healthy growth—difficulties, frustrations, impossibilities, for "when I am weak, then I am strong": "in hopeless circumstances he hopefully believed."

And they came. There is no need to go into them in detail! Days of agony and darkness. Days when one's life's work seemed in ruin around one, when the mission one loved seemed collapsing, when the hand of practically all friends and fellow Christians seemed against a tiny remnant of us. And I myself, with my wife, was called to take a stand completely alone, on behalf of the few on the field, surrounded by criticism and fierce opposition.

Then in the travail, I cannot tell how (indeed I have learned that one usually cannot trace the "how" of God's deepest dealings), what I had seen and rejoiced in in theory became my own in practice. I saw how to walk the broad road of faith, how to have and maintain that touch with God, that living fruitful union with Him which in infinite grace and condescension He has given us as our inheritance in Christ; and we began to go that way.

Fifteen more years have now passed, years when, by God's grace, these vital principles have been ever more strongly built into one's life. Others, many others, have learned them, practised them, and rejoice with us to see the marvellous truth of them in their concrete result. In the ranks of the Crusade, tremendous transformations have taken place: God's work has forged ahead, increased and abounded: souls have been saved world-wide: tens of thousands have heard the Gospel who had never before heard the blessed Name: Christians by the hundred have been revived and stirred into action: Christ Himself has become increasingly the all in all; all fresh springs have been found in Him; all hunger and thirst satisfied according to His Word; desire increased beyond measure that He only should be glorified; His Word become the joy and rejoicing of the heart.

Details need not be given, for this is no place for them: but gradually this truth and that, concerning the inner life abiding in Christ, and the outer life of service in His name, have fitted into place, have been tested, examined, adjusted. Much has been learned by failures, and some things remain inexplicable: until the time seems to have come to try and put on paper something of what one has learned. "To the law and to the testimony: if they speak not according to this word, it is because there is no light in them." That is the touchstone. We believe that the Scriptures are God's final revelation to man, the words that He speaks which are spirit and life; and all that we say here is only reliable in so far as it is an exposition of God's revealed truth. This is not autobiography. It is to be a humble examination of faith, what it is and how it works. It seemed necessary, however, to give this brief preliminary sketch of how and why such as I, who am not a trained theologian but a missionary secretary, should write on such a subject. It is just my contribution, I trust to God's glory, of one ray of God's truth which has steadily shone in my heart and on my pathway these twenty-five years.

Chapter Two

FAITH A NATURAL FACULTY

WE will start at the beginning. One of the chief hindrances to the understanding and exercise of faith is the separation in our thinking between the natural and spiritual, due to the fall. There is a flesh and there is Spirit. Flesh draws upon one set of energies, Spirit upon another. Faith, it is argued, belongs to the realm of the Spirit. It is a "gift of God", and therefore can only be exercised under divine stimulation. We must pray for it ("Lord, increase our faith"), wait for it, use it only according as God has dealt to us the measure of faith. When and where it is not thus given, we are helpless, becalmed, immobile.

A grave misapprehension lies at the root of this devitalizing outlook. How did God make man? A living soul, we are told, in His own image: that is to say, with all the attributes of personality. A man feels and desires: he thinks, he wills, he speaks, he acts. All these marvellous faculties combine to make a person; but the point to note is that in themselves they are neutral powers. They are neither good nor evil: they are the raw material of human nature, the mighty forces directed to weal or woe by the spirit that is in man. To love, to hate; to admire, to despise; to boast, to be humble; to be angry, to be calm; to have fear, to have faith; to be stern, to be gentle; any of these can be right, any can be wrong. They are the elemental gifts of God in nature to His human offspring. By these men are made "after the similitude ᴐf God", and by them they walk the course of this world. What matters is, do they walk after the flesh, or after the Spirit?

It will be seen later that a proper grasp of the neutral condition of this raw material of human nature, and its relationship to the spirit that controls it, gives the key to the understanding of many problems concerning the walk and warfare of a Christian, the understanding, conquest and proper use of temptation, release from false condemnation, proper discernment between flesh and Spirit, the solution to the vexed problems of sanctification. These we will examine later on. But at the moment we will concentrate on this one point. Amongst the major faculties with which human nature is basically endowed, is faith. The greatest faculty of all is love. God is love. The whole creation is God's love manifested in innumerable forms. All is love, or love in its reverse form, hate. Love is the consuming fire, which is God. Man is love likewise, perverted or purified. Love of the world or love of the Father must dominate the human heart; he must love, for he *is* love. He loves long before he is redeemed. He loves from the time he becomes a living soul. But what does he love?

Next to love in importance comes faith. Love is the driving force. Desire (love pure or perverted) controls, contrives, creates all that ever comes to pass. Emotion, not reason, is at humanity's helm. Love motivates, but faith acts. Faith *is* action. By faith alone can a man act. Faith carries out the urges of love. Faith works by love.

Consider the importance of faith. Consider its place in human behaviour. Is there one single act that one single man has ever taken, from the trivial to the sublime, which has not love as its driving force, and faith as its method of performance? A man eats. Why? Because he wants to. Love, desire, is the motive power. How then does he eat, and what? He sees some food which is both pleasant and nutritious, he believes in its value; he takes, masticates, swallows, digests, every action of which is pure faith and nothing but faith. At any moment in any of these actions, if his faith in the food were shaken, if he were caused to change his faith into its reverse—believing that it was bad for him—he would immediately and automatically cease to take, masticate, swallow, or even digest (if he could!). Faith *is* human action. Faith is the God-implanted, natural and only way by which a man can go through all the processes of doing or obtaining the things he desires.

And, by implication, if man is made in the image of God, and if man's fundamental God-given faculties are those of love and faith, they are also God's ways of action, even of creation. The Scripture gives plain indication of this, and it has its importance when we carry the examination of faith still further.

Apply this formula of faith to every single human action, from breathing right up the scale to great scientific discoveries, and, finally, across the gulf to the realm of the Spirit; and it will be seen that there is no other conceivable method of human activity. A purchase in a shop, taking a seat on a chair, breathing a breath, picking up an article, all are sheer acts of faith. Likewise, historic achievements, such as the discovery of radium. Certain investigations, we read, drew Mme. Curie's attention to the probability of another element, not yet known to science, in a material called pitchblende, a throw-out from certain Austrian mines. The more she investigates, the more the conviction grows. Her fellow-scientists scoff, but she believes. She feels sure that the evidence justifies such faith. But living faith is action, only dead faith has no works accompanying it. So, quietly, secretly, she and her husband put all the money they can spare into buying truckloads of pitchblende and having them brought to the hut at the back of their house. There they labour, one year, two years, until one evening she calls her husband into their home-made laboratory, and there for the first time in history is seen the glowing tube of radium. Here is natural faith, inherent faith, inspired by the glimpse of a scientific truth, directed to a natural, so-called secular objective; but it is a higher type of faith, or rather a higher form of the exercise of faith, than such simple acts as eating, breathing, sitting: for, in this case, the object of faith was by no means so self-evident; some indeed ridiculed it; it took time and careful study to come to a conviction solid enough to justify the decisive action which is faith: and when the decision to act had been made, it took time, patience, self-denial, for the hypothesis of faith to be demonstrated as fact. And equally, it will be seen, as we move on to things spiritual, that in the realm of the Spirit there are simpler, more obvious stimuli to faith; and more advanced, more exacting forms of its exercise.

That faith is an inherent capacity in all men is also made plain in the Scriptures. "Cursed is he that *trusteth* in man." "Put not your trust in princes." "Trust not in uncertain riches." "Because thou has relied on the King of Syria, and not relied on the Lord thy God ..."

Sufficient, I hope, has now been said to bring home this first point of fundamental importance: that faith is a natural faculty of man: that, next to love, it is the most important faculty that man possesses, for faith is the core of decisive action: that man, while he lives and breathes, can never cease exercising faith, and has never performed one single action in the world's history which is not energized by faith: that to seek faith or ask for faith is as ridiculous as asking for lungs to breathe with, or mouth to eat with. Man is compounded of faith, and can do no other than exercise it in one direction or another.

Chapter Three

FROM NATURAL TO SPIRITUAL FAITH

WHERE now comes the connection or difference between natural and spiritual faith? There is no difference.[1] There are no two sorts of faith to be connected, for, in both realms, it is the exercise of the one and only God-implanted faculty of faith. The difference is merely in the object of faith. But here there is a difference so radical that it might appear as if there were two altogether different types of faith.

It is obvious that man was created by God to be a spiritual being. God is spirit, Jesus Himself said, and He is "the Father of spirits". In other words, the things of the Spirit were meant to be natural to man, not supernatural. They were meant to be his normal environment. The pure "see" God. Had man remained pure, by the faculty of this spirit indwelt by God's Spirit, he would have been as accustomed to the spiritual "sight" of God as his natural eyes are to the things of this world; a condition indeed which is fulfilled in varying measure by those who have

---

[1] If the question is asked, what about such a text as Eph. 2: 8: "For by grace are ye saved through faith; and that not of yourselves: it is the gift of God"; or in 2 Peter 1: 1: "To them that have obtained like precious faith with us"? The answer is that all have the *capacity* to believe; but actual faith is that capacity stimulated to action by a faith-producing object. In this sense Scriptural or spiritual faith—the act of believing in Christ—is a gift of God, for it could not exist without Christ as its all-satisfying object. But it remains equally true that the capacity to believe is inherent in all; otherwise God could not command us to believe, as He does.

been purified by the blood of Christ, who have been born of His Spirit, and thus "see" His kingdom.

Owing to the fall, however, spiritual sight became unnatural. Man became dead toward God, blind to His kingdom, and only the things of time and sense remained as his natural realm.

Now faith starts by seeing a thing, in which it thus can naturally and effortlessly believe. A man sees a book; it does not take him a split second, not the faintest conscious effort, to believe that it is a book and that he can pick it up and read it. Yet all those reactions are actually the first forms of faith. The book has stimulated his faith-faculty, and the man performs an act of living faith if he takes the book up and reads it.

Thus in the normal acts of life the process of living faith is so natural, so unnoticed, so continual, that no one dreams of calling it faith—but it is.

Now, however, we have a gulf to cross, a chasm which man cannot bridge, from the natural to the spiritual, from the land of man's exile back into the paradise from which long ago the flaming sword barred him. How can faith leap that gulf? And, again, is the same quality of faith effectual on both banks?

God, not man, has bridged that gulf, and bridged it for the one purpose of reclaiming, redeeming to Himself, back from the devil, back from the flesh, back from the world, man with his two dynamic faculties, productive of so much evil or so much good, those faculties of love and faith.

God Himself entered the human arena by the one act of matchless grace in sending His beloved Son in the likeness of sinful flesh and as a sacrifice for sin. And in doing this, He took every possible means that could be taken to quicken love and stimulate faith in Himself. In order to act, faith must first see. Very well then, God will meet faith on its own ground. First, there remains in man, even at the fall, the moral sense, the conscience, the law written in the heart, the capacity of knowing right from wrong, of recognizing the highest, of thirsting after his lost perfection. These God then stimulates through history by revelations of truth, accompanied by mighty works of deliverance, by His dealings with His chosen people, all rays and foreshadowings of the true light which was to shine, all material for a truth-seeking faith. Then comes the moment, in the fullness of time, when the true light shines out in the darkness, the Word is made flesh and dwells among us, full of grace and truth. His incomparable words, His deeds, His symbolic acts of giving the bread and wine, His victorious redeeming death, His carefully attested resurrection, His appearances, His visible ascension, the coming of the Spirit, the transformed followers, their written records, peak on peak, form the mighty mountain range of visual testimony.

And so God comes down to meet man's faith, with His Son, His Word, His Spirit. The gulf is bridged. Faith can operate in the realm of the Kingdom of Heaven as simply and naturally as in the things of earth.

Let us note in passing, however, lest we get things out of proportion, the relative importance of giver and recipient in this matter of faith. Faith, in itself, which is the capacity to receive, to use, to apply, is utterly useless unless the material is first provided upon which it can be exercised. What use are mouth and stomach, unless there be food? What use lungs, unless there be air? God's wondrous order in nature and spirit is very simple. He, the Giver, has provided all. In one ceaseless river He pours His gifts upon us, all things natural and supernatural, whether it be sun and rain, food and the riches of the earth, or the grace in Christ Jesus. All in unending abundance for body and soul is ours. All things but one. He does not force acceptance on us. He does not compel us to live, whether in body or spirit. Love seeks for love, free, unconditioned, love for love's sake. Therefore God made man in His image, free in will and choice, able to accept, able to reject; for God seeks the worship, love and service of willing hearts. He gives, He presses all upon us, His gifts, His Son, Himself. But we must take. Food He provides, but we must take and eat. Air, but we must breathe. Ninety-nine per cent of life consists of God's endless giving. One per cent consists of taking. Both are essential, but in that proportion. We are here stressing faith, for our object is to analyse and examine the way man receives and uses what he is given. That is not meant to give glory to faith or credit to faith, as if faith produced anything. Laith supplies the one per cent. That is all. God supplies the 99 per cent—to Him is the glory, in Him is the grace, for Him is our love. (Indeed, properly speaking, the 100 per cent is His, for faith itself is a God-given, natural faculty.) Our consideration is only centred round the one per cent, yet that must be considered just because experience shows that so many Christians flounder about, not because they do not know the grace of God revealed in Christ, but because they do not know how, steadily, consistently, to appropriate, use, and apply what they are given, according to the set laws of appropriation—of faith.

And now let us watch this process of faith as it passes from its exercise in the natural to the supernatural. What happens when the Spirit of God brings conviction of sin? It is obvious. He penetrates the thick walls of our self-righteousness. Every man by nature has built around him some working philosophy of life. He is as good as other folk. He does not do his neighbour any harm. He believes in a Creator who is love, so hell is unthinkable, and all will be right. Or else he has a frankly materialistic and hedonistic, or agnostic, or even atheistic, point of view. Anyhow, he has some basis to life, however flimsy, however unsatisfactory, or however self-satisfying. And to that basis his faith is attached. He is a believer all right—in his particular outlook: it may be a false faith, a perverted faith, but it is his faith.

Now, conviction of sin knocks that flimsy prop from under him. It no longer satisfies, it is no longer reliable. He sees through it: all his righteousnesses are as filthy rags: his sins are ever before him: he has hewn him cisterns, broken cisterns, that can hold no water. Now his faith is at sea, tossed hither and thither, with nothing left for it to take hold of. Where can it ground its anchor?

The Spirit points to Jesus. The Spirit and the Bride say, Come. The Word speaks its message, "Look unto Me and be ye saved". "Him that cometh unto Me I will in no wise cast out": "He that believeth on me hath everlasting life." Here is faith's sure resting-place. Here is its rock of ages— Jesus, the Son of God.

The decision is made, Christ for me: "Nothing in my hand I bring, simply to thy Cross I cling." Faith dares to take Him at His word: "The Lord is my shepherd": "My Beloved is Mine and I am His." Not a new faculty of faith, mind you, but a new content for faith. That's all. The very same faith which was once centred in the man's own righteousness is now torn from that false embrace to rest itself upon "that which is through faith of Christ, the righteousness which is of God by faith". A natural faculty purified, redirected, possessed and controlled by the Spirit.

And let us note that the one per cent of human faith had

to go out to meet the 99 per cent of God's grace. Without this, not all the conviction in the world, not all the sorrow for sin, the change of mind, the prayers and tears and resolutions, could bring the sinner to the enjoyment of that grace. The central faculty of faith had to be exercised, that faculty which is personality in action. The man who had chosen to believe in a false philosophy of life, who had acted out his faith by his self-pleasing, self-confident way of life, had now by an equally deliberate choice to reject that philosophy as a basis for his faith, and by that same faith to accept Jesus in all the fullness of His forgiveness, mercy and renewal. The faith could not save, only His abounding grace could do that; but the faith was the decisive action of a free person, seeing, believing, receiving, and opening his being to the control of Jesus Christ, his new-found Lord.

Chapter Four

WE said before, concerning natural faith, that there are two kinds: simple and advanced. One seems almost effortless, almost automatic; the other calls for concentration, adventure, persistence. It is the same in the life of the Spirit.

Saving faith is very simple. "Except ye become as a little child, ye cannot enter." A man sees his need, sees his Saviour, takes him at His word, confesses Him, and lo. Christ is his; he knows it, he has the witness in himself, the Spirit Himself bears witness with his spirit that he is a child of God. His faith is consummated, for perfected faith possesses, and knows it possesses. It is as simple as the eating of bread or drinking of water.

The probable reason for this simplicity and ease of reception is that man can much more easily believe a thing that concerns the past or future than the present. When he comes to Jesus as a sinner, his main preoccupation is usually his past sins and their consequences, or his future destiny: past and future, rather than the present; and it is not very hard to take Christ at His word, that the past is blotted out in His blood and the future assured in His gift of eternal life.

But it is not long before a far more serious problem arises, more serious, that is to say, in the difficulty of its solution. As time passes, the young Christian becomes more and more conscious of the dead weight of his own corrupt nature. Truth can only be revealed to us in stages, as we become capable of accepting it, truth about ourselves and corresponding truth about the fullness of deliverance in Christ. At first we see sins rather than sin. We are made conscious that we are lost and defiled, but that is interpreted to us by our conscience more in the light of the sins we have committed and the attitudes of rebellion and indifference which we have adopted, than by a sight of the sinful nature which has produced all these evil fruits. At first we see outwardly, rather than inwardly. Equally our first consciousness of cleansing is from outward defilements such as these; as "Christian" in *Pilgrim's Progress*, we know our sins as a load on our backs, and rejoice as the burden tumbles off at the Cross and rolls down into the empty tomb.

A further, but not final, stage in self-revelation and deliverance comes to many when they have their eyes opened to see what a hold the world has upon their affections. It might be called the stage of separation or consecration. Man is so made that he may have a multitude of interests, each of which has some claim upon his heart; but down in the centre there is always one master-interest, one master-passion. The heart of man, like a wheel, has many spokes, but one hub. That is what is meant by the constant emphasis in the Scriptures on the word "heart". It is the focal point of personality. When a man does a thing with all his heart, his enthusiasm is in it: his will, his affection, his imagination—himself. "Keep thy heart with all diligence," says the wise man, "for out of it are the issues of life." Where a man's heart is, he is. And a man's heart is always centred somewhere. In its long, blind quest for its true Owner, the Beloved for whom it was made, it may flit from thing to thing, from passing interest to passing interest, or may twine firmly and fast round one object. The heart is held by what it holds. What a man possesses, possesses him. It is his idol and his master. This is the true meaning of the accursed thing the Bible calls idolatry. It is that thing which has mastered the heart and claims the centre of its affections, that heart which by right of creation and redemption belongs solely to Him who made it for Himself. "No man can serve two masters", said Christ: but he is always serving one, he is never without a master of some kind.

Before conversion it may be something gross, evil—sensual pleasures, dishonest practices, unscrupulous ambition. After conversion it certainly cannot be these, for he that is born of God does not keep sinning. But there may still be an "inordinate affection" for something innocent in itself, something which is useful, helpful, uplifting, if retained in the circumference of the affections, but a destructive idol if in the centre. It might be, and often is, a person, a loved one, and Jesus' warning voice is heard in those terrific words: "If any man hate not . . . he cannot be my disciple." It may be business interests, home, the pursuit of knowledge, politics, sport, society. It may be any of these good things of life which we are given richly to enjoy, but not to adore and worship, not to hold or be held by in such entwining bonds that we cannot do without them.

Then to the younger Christian, or to the older maybe who has lost the first engrossing love for Christ, comes the rapier thrust of conviction: "Lovest thou me more than these?" And it is borne in on us with a burning, smarting certainty that something is more to us than Christ. As C. T. Studd once said about his own early period of backsliding: " You can always tell where a man's heart is. What moves the heart, wags the tongue! I used to take every opportunity I could to speak of Christ. Then cricket came into the foreground, and Christ in the background, and I was talking cricket." Idolatry. And we doubt whether there is a single soul who walks the pilgrim way with God but the same discovery comes to him with devastating effect at some time or other; the precious citadel of his heart has opened its gates to someone, something, other than God. A usurper reigns there, be it as sacred a person as mother, sweetheart, husband, wife: and the idol must be cast down and cast out.

A ruthless struggle ensues. Every subtle argument is used to justify the retention of both. A share of the throne for Christ and a share for that other. But "My glory will I not give to another." Thank God, He will take no compromise. Thank God, He is jealous, as well as patient. He will be Lord of all or not Lord at all. And the reason is easy to see, after the battle is won and the surrender made, though not at all obvious to the storm-tossed soul in the throes of its life and death wrestling. What holds the heart absorbs and occupies all the energies of a man. Around that thing he thinks, enthuses, has his daydreams, plans and acts. Again we hear the word of Solomon: "Keep thy heart with all diligence." If, therefore, the heart is set on something selfish, limited, local, all man's God-endowed energies are centred round that temporal, trivial, personal interest. But God has made man to be universal, to have all things, to love all things, to serve all things.[1] He is to be as wide in his outreach, in his sympathies, in his activities, as his Saviour. Is he not joint heir with Christ, the heir of all things? Are not all things his: the world, life, things present and things to come? Is he not even to judge

---

[1] "Disciplined Tenderness" (a phrase borrowed from my friend, Jock Purves), is the beautiful fruit of a God-centred life. And we might add disciplined delight in all things, disciplined use of all things, disciplined appreciation of all things. It is the fruition of the perfect *law* of liberty. All is "in temperature" as the old mystic said, when Christ is the life-centre.

angels? Can such a one be parochially minded? Firmly, faithfully, must his grip be released from all inordinate affections; from too strong loves for special men and things, from every neatly disguised idol.

That he might be crippled, dispossessed, stripped? Does God delight in limitations, suppressions, negations? No, indeed, but that he might be filled with all the fullness of God, by having God alone in the centre of his heart, Christ only as his master-passion, and then, possessing God, he possesses all things. Does he regain what he lost? Let the poet answer: "All which I took from thee I did but take, not for thy harms, but just that thou mightest seek it in My arms. All which thy child's mistake fancies as lost, I have stored for thee at home. Rise, clasp My hand, and come!"

Chapter Five

Sin lies deeper than sins which are the outward form it takes; deeper than world attachments, which are the golden chain of its subtle enslavement. Sin is the root, sins are the fruit. Sin's dwelling place is in the ego ("the sin that dwelleth in me"), in the centre of the personality, in the heart. Sin reveals itself in its subtlest shades in all kinds of manifestations of the self life. So undiscernible are they to any but God-enlightened eyes, that the writer to the Hebrews speaks of the word of God being sharp enough to pierce even to the dividing asunder of soul and spirit, to the discerning of the thoughts and intents of the heart. Only the Holy Spirit can convict a man of his outward sins: only the Holy Spirit can show him his secret idolatries. How much more is it true that only the Holy Spirit can expose sin to its roots right in the inner ego of a man!

That was the complete catastrophe of the fall. The ego, the heart, was created as God's dwelling-place, the holy of holies where the universal Spirit of goodness, beauty and truth, would hold converse with man's created spirit, dwell in blessed union and communion with him, be the light of his eyes, the wisdom of his mind, the strength of his will, unfold to him all the hidden glories of God's creation. Man, foolish, beguiled, self-seeking, deliberately took the frightful step of rejecting the gentle dominion of the Father of Spirits, and surrendering the throne of his personality to that impudent, usurping tyrant, his own independent self. What a harvest of horror he has reaped—selfishness, pride, lust, wrath, hatred, malice, war, disease, death. And, hidden behind the supposed dominion of king ego, there has lurked the all-pervading spirit of evil, that spirit which Paul says works in the children of disobedience.

Such has been man's condition, all his magnificent faculties, which were created for God's use and God's glory, enslaved, infected, defiled by the dominion of his rebel self, all together forming the "I" that is carnal, the flesh in which dwelleth no good thing, the old man corrupt according to the deceitful lusts. Yet that rebel self may display much of the common goodness still existing in God's creation, the goodness of which Jesus speaks, when He says that sinners do good to those that do good to them, and that the evil know how to give good gifts to their children: it may do kind acts; be cheerful; be polished; be clever. And even when Christ has been welcomed within, in humble penitence as Lord of the life, that old self, largely unrecognized, will still reveal its presence in a thousand ways by self-will, self-importance, self-sufficiency; or alternatively by a self-consciousness that is bondage, or a self-depreciation that paralyses.

It seems that God's Spirit has to take every forward-moving soul through a drastic process of self-exposure. That undiscovered self-principle lurking in the depths, that root of sin, has to be looked in the face. Its presumptuous claim to be a sufficient source of wisdom and ability has to be exposed in its falsity. Its save-yourself attitude has to be recognized and rejected. And such knowledge can only come through failure, through humiliation, through despair. Then, and then only, is the soul ripe for that inner leap of faith: the dying of the old, the rising of the new, the full and final enthronement of its proper Lord.

What trouble God took to bring this one truth home to all who would wholly follow Him. They had to learn it. It was the key to a God-lit life.

Abraham took fourteen years after his first great step of obedience and consecration when "he went out, not knowing whither he went". Twice over, in the flight to Egypt and the advice of Sarah, his subtle old self swept him off his feet; first in a panicky effort to save his own skin, and second by preferring the advice of his wife to the plain word of God. By these two excursions into by-path meadow, the hidden existence of his fallen self was exposed to him in its two main centres of entrenchment, through the body and mind. At last he was in a condition of brokenness, in which God could speak to him that word of final deliverance: "Walk before Me and be thou perfect"; and a mighty exploit of the Spirit was set in motion which became the standard act of faith throughout all history.

Jacob's history in this respect is one of the best known in the Bible, although it is also true that he is greatly maligned and his true character unappreciated. Fallen nature prefers Esau to Jacob any day, but not so God. And the reason is obvious. Esau was a rank materialist, sensual, worldly, selfish, a heartbreak to his parents. God cannot but "hate" such, for by their free choice they are the antagonists of the only two laws which can ever turn this world from a hell to a heaven: the love of God with all our heart, and the love of our neighbour as ourself. Yet Esau was dressed in outer garments sufficiently attractive almost to deceive the elect, with social charms, good looks, athletic grace and prowess, and a certain abandon and open-handedness that worldlings often have.

Not so Jacob. Cautious, crafty, stay-at-home, there is little to appeal about him, but one thing—and that only

God and his mother could see. He believed in God. In his own crabbed way he loved God. God and His promises, which Esau would barter for a bowl of beans, were so real to Jacob that, with all the intensity of an intense nature, he set himself to obtain them. This, perhaps, was why God called Himself the God of Jacob; not because He has mercy on the crooked, but because He is ever found of those who seek Him with the whole heart. But what a dominant "I", what a scheming, bargaining self! Obvious enough to all except the possessor! It took twenty-one years for Jacob to make the discovery that his one enemy was his own uncrucified ego. Tricking and tricked, still he did not see that it was self he was trusting. There remained one trump card, and God played that. He knows just when and where to give the *coup de grâce*, for He knows our soft spots. One fear Jacob never conquered, and that was the sworn vengeance of his brother. Wild horses would not drag him back within his reach. But God's voice came to him, "Return"; and, deeper than all his schemes and fears, one voice had the last word with him. He was God's, and it is important to note that these deeper dealings of the Spirit are only possible in lives which are first so wholly given to God that when the pinch comes they will take anything He gives them and go anywhere He sends them. So back he went. Every wile that his scheming brain could devise was made ready to placate Esau. But well he knew that such would be but as straw to a whirlwind. Was not Esau coming with four hundred men to make no mistake about it? That night, alone at Jabbok, the real fight was fought, not with his outward enemy—for outward things are not really our enemies at all—but with his inner, that unrealized, unbroken, self. Set, as he was, somehow still to scheme some final clever getaway, filled with his own thoughts, far too preoccupied to think of transferring his trust to God, the Lord Himself could do nothing with him, until his very body cracked under the strain. Lame and helpless, at last the light dawned, self was seen in its true colours; and all the energies of that intense personality which for twenty-one years had centred in his own scheming, turned from himself, helpless and broken, and clave with a like intensity to his God. "I will not let *Thee* go except Thou bless me." He was through. "As a prince hast thou power with God and with men, and hast prevailed." And next day the avenger who came to slay him met him with embraces!

Joseph, that holy and consecrated young life, precious to the Lord as are all who are pure from their youth up, is sometimes foolishly portrayed as a conceited and pampered young fledgling. A thousand miles from it! Morally mature and courageous, he stood undefiled alone amongst his brethren, although it may not perhaps have been his business to expose them to their father. Rarely can God entrust a vision of greatness to a mere stripling, but He did to young Joseph. Again he overstepped the mark in telling it to father and brothers; but the father, who well knew God and His ways, even while rebuking his son, sensed the Divine origin of the dreams and took good note of them.

But it was the same old story—Joseph consecrated, holy, fearless; but, mingled with this, the self-assurance and self-righteousness of the unsanctified ego. Tremendous fires had to do their purifying work to fit them for tremendous responsibilities. Consecrated but uncrucified self could never stand the dizzy and desperately dangerous heights for which he was destined. So down he was taken for fourteen years, down, down, first to slavery to which he was sold by his own brethren, then to the dungeon, falsely stained with the vilest of accusations; and, even then, when it seemed that a word to Pharaoh from a grateful heart might relieve him, left to rot in forgetfulness. Could God still be with him? We wonder that Joseph did not curse God and become an atheist. The iron entered into his soul. But faith held. That was all he had left to him—naked faith; and by that golden thread he steadied himself, received the blows as from God, found favour with Him, did his servile tasks with a willing heart, and, clad in the armour of God's living presence, triumphed over inward resentment and the outward appeals of flattery and sensuality. A character indeed sanctified, meet for the Master's use; a self, purged of itself, able to live in the glittering and sinful surroundings of a heathen metropolis, married to the daughter of a heathen priest, yet walking with God in white, bearing a witness to the true God which reached from the palace to the humblest cottage.

Chapter Six

UNDISCOVERED SELF (2)

In Moses', more than in any other life, is the necessity of self-exposure clearly seen. How complete was his consecration; rank, wealth, pleasure, coolly and deliberately rejected for the greater honour of suffering affliction with the people of God, and the greater riches of the reproach of Christ. The Scriptures contain no more magnificent description of a dedicated life than Hebrews 11 : 24-26. Yet that same man was a helpless fugitive a few weeks later, his plans for leading Israel out of their bondage shattered to a thousand bits. No power in that consecration! One might surely have thought that God would stand by such a man and scatter his enemies. But no. It was his enemies that scattered him. It had to be. For not even God Himself can be the strength of a man, not even God Himself can lead him forward in triumph, until that false usurper, who has planted himself in every man's heart since the fall, is cast out. Moses had left his sin and left the world, but he hadn't left himself. "Learned in all the wisdom of the Egyptians, mighty in words and in deeds, he supposed his brethren would have understood how that God by his hand would deliver them." Exactly. Moses had one enemy left, one hindrance to power, and that was—Moses.

And so, with Jacob and Joseph and many another, he had to tread the long, long trail of self-exposure, out in his case to the backside of the desert, to do the one job which an Egyptian execrated—shepherding. Truly the way to God is down, not up. It lies through the valley of humiliation. Blessed valley. It leads to the heights, but is the only trail to them.

But, as with others, Moses could take it. For these are not lessons for the rebellious. They are the secret things to be learned only by the whole-hearted. So when the winds blow and the floods come, the house is seen to be founded on a rock, the rock of a genuine surrender. If God wills it so, well, it all seems utter confusion to a Joseph or Moses, but painful though it is, they accept it. For them it is God first, at any price. Though He slay them, they will trust in Him; and the key to those forty years which Moses spent in the desert was the statement that he "was content to dwell with the man (Jethro)". So God could work in that yielded, puzzled heart, and every shred of the flesh could be cauterized in those lonely years of heart-searching. True, faith did not die, the faith that God could and would deliver His people, but faith in himself had its thorough funeral.

Then came the moment, the revelation of the permanent presence of the I AM, in the fire that never went out, the commission to a shrinking Moses (how changed from forty years before), the provision of the rod of faith. In one day the pygmy within had become a giant without, whereas forty years ago the seeming giant within was proved to be a pygmy without. God had joined Himself to that humbled, finite self. There was now room for Him. He, who is really always there in all the resources of the I AM, could not then be seen and felt and known, for a self-sufficient ego filled the foreground. Now the vision was cleared—not I, but Jehovah, the I AM, the all-sufficient. Now, that brilliant brain and that character trained to leadership was available for God, for the purpose for which He had predestined him; for God is preparing His instruments in brain and hand long before

37

they know Him, that in the fullness of time, lifted out of themselves and into Him, these years of training and special abilities might be put to the use of His Kingdom. Did not God say to the young Jeremiah: "Before I formed thee I knew thee; and before thou camest forth out of the womb I sanctified thee, and I ordained thee a prophet unto the nations"; and to Paul, that it was God who had separated him from his mother's womb and called him by His grace?

What a man came back from Midian to Egypt! A child within in simple and humble dependence upon God, but a "god" without;[1] the fugitive became a pursuer; a leader, rejected in the tinsel display of his own superiority, now revered and followed in the anointing of the Holy Spirit; a man who could not find enough power in his God to save him from the first threat of danger, now wielding all heaven's resources to rescue a nation, paralyse an opposing empire, feed two million for forty years, and give them moral laws which have been the foundation of a world civilization.

We must hasten on, passing by many an outstanding character whose history teaches the same lesson. There was Joshua, learning his first lesson against the Amalekites that his own generalship was not enough; then descending from commanding an army to being Moses' servant for forty years; then coming to his life's crisis, his brook Jabbok, on the return of the twelve spies, when he decided, after a night's hesitation, that God, not human opinion, was to be his trust (for this was doubtless the reason why, on their first report to Moses, only Caleb protested against their pessimistic outlook; but a day later was joined by Joshua in his isolated stand); and, finally, knowing his God and doing exploits from the death of Moses onward, God now using his natural gifts of mili-

[1] Exod. 7: 1.

38

tary leadership purged from their self-sufficient bias. Then we have David, holy in his youth like Joseph, daring in his boyhood faith, performer as a young man of a national exploit of faith as magnificent as any in history, and showing all the evidences of one who has found the key to the proper use of faith.[1] But not really so. The fierce fires of testing through Saul soon found him wanting and showed that the same old enemy, in David, had to be exposed and dealt with, as in all the rest. David took charge, not God, as he listened to Michal's panicky advice (it was Abraham and Sarah over again); fugitive in a cave for eight years, the heart knew its own bitterness, till, once for all, David gave his self up, died and rose again, as in that hour of desperate distress at Ziklag he turned from his own tears and fears to "encourage himself in the Lord his God". A new David mounted the throne a few weeks later. Not David indeed who could not fall, that is another matter for later examination, but a David whose reign to the glory of God has been unequalled in history.

Think of Elisha, so happy in his youthful consecration, making a farewell feast before he left all to follow Elijah; and Elisha, twelve years later, a desperate seeker and suppliant. For what? The spirit of Elijah. Those intervening years had shown him that consecration was not enough. He must know the secret of Elijah's power with God, if he was to be Elijah's successor. In other words, self-confidence had to die. In desperation he sought: "As the Lord liveth and as thy soul liveth, I will not leave thee." And God meets the desperate. The heavenly vision

[1] 1 Sam. 17 is a perfect example in all its stages of a victory of faith; yet it only turned out to be what in sporting terms would be called "a beginner's luck", for David yet had much to learn of himself in the valley of humiliation before, from Ziklag onwards (1 Sam. 30), David's Jabbok, he became an adept in the ways of the Spirit.

was opened to him, "My father, my father, the chariots of Israel had the horsemen thereof." He learned and grasped his resources in the Lord of hosts, and the bewildered seeker became the ready dispenser of the grace and power of God. The one who saw the chariots of the Lord at Elijah's departure lived in that ever-present reality, and could at once see them around him without effort, fear or doubting, in beleaguered Dothan. "Alas, master, what shall we do?" cries out his terrified servant. "Fear not," at once he answers, for "they that be with us are more than they that be with them." "Lord, open the young man's eyes that he may see." And he saw "the mountain was full of horses and chariots of fire round about Elisha". Here is the inner victory, the birth and progress of a faith that overcomes the world.

The New Testament is not so prodigal in vivid character sketches as the Old; but two or three teach us just the same truths. It is most interesting to note that the early days of the Saviour, perfect Man as well as God, give the same indication of a definite attitude that had to be taken towards self; though, in His case, of course, "without sin"; and this fact in itself is an interesting pointer to the truth that the human self is not sin, only the poisoned, fallen self of unregenerate man—a truth we probe into later. We read that He "increased in wisdom and stature", and that He "waxed strong in spirit", indicating that in all three realms—spirit, soul (mind) and body—there was growth. A stage in that development was plainly the scene of the visit to Jerusalem, the three days spent with the Rabbis in the temple, and the surprised exclamation to his parents: "Wist ye not that I must be about my Father's business?" Clearly it had not occurred to Him that He was offending and giving anxiety to those whose charge He still was. To Him, the Father's business was all that mattered, but in came the warning note. Does that "must" come from the Father? Has the divine call yet come for the public ministry? Without hesitation, without a moment's inner conflict, He rendered perfect obedience, returned with His parents, was "subject unto them" another eighteen years. He "learned obedience". He worked out as a Man the perfect submission and interaction of the self-life with its true Indweller. He went the way of probation and self-abnegation that Adam failed to go, which was to have had its consummation at the Tree of Life. By Him, that was realized in the descent of the Holy Spirit like a dove upon Him. It was the full sunlight of realized union. "This is my beloved Son." "I and My Father are One." "The Spirit of the Lord is upon Me." And, in the glorious ministry which followed, no emphasis of His was stronger than upon the fact that "the Son can do nothing of Himself"; "I came not to do My own will" "The words that I speak, I speak not of Myself"; "I came not of Myself". Always it was "The Father that sent me", "He that sent Me", "I do always those things that please Him". Total self-emptying, total God-filling: and, in that holy and perfect relationship, the greatest life was lived in three years that ever has been, or can be, lived; the greatest words spoken, the greatest death died. How plainly the lesson comes home; self-realization begins, continues and ends with self-emptying.

Peter, the last we look at, was a plain instance. How wholehearted was his consecration: "Lo, we have left all"; "I will lay down my life for Thy sake." "Peter, Peter, you don't know yourself; you don't see that self-confidence is your snare and downfall. You must learn by disaster. But I have prayed for you that your faith fail not." The same old trouble, undiscovered self, and it took a big crash to bring the fact home. But, there again, as with the other men of old, Peter's heart was in the right place. If he failed momentarily, he still loved; and because he loved, he wept bitterly. The lesson was learned, a chastened Peter came forth; and when the Holy Ghost fell, He could take that warm heart, that bold tongue, that courageous spirit, freed now from self, and use it as His mouthpiece to the world.

Chapter Seven

THE LAW OF TRANSMUTATION

WE have not scrupled to show in some detail the ramifications of the independent self in the most earnest of God's servants. We have done so because a thorough insight into our own nature is the essential preliminary to a vital experience of "the law of the Spirit of life in Christ Jesus" which makes us free from the law of sin and death. This also is the Scriptural order and emphasis. We are set the standard in Romans 6; are given the facts about the self-line in Romans 7; and experience the deliverance in Romans 8.

But one point needs to be stressed as a possible corrective. In all these Bible characters which have been cited, the exposure of the flesh has been a long task. This might well put an earnest reader into bondage. "I suppose", he might say, "I must expect a six or ten years period during which my true condition is brought home to me." Not so indeed. Let us say it with emphasis. There is one great difference between these men of God and ourselves. They lived the other side of the Cross before the Saviour and the Apostle Paul. What Christ did for us, Paul, more than any other writer, was God's mouthpiece for expounding, and without doubt he himself in his own soul's experience, probably in Arabia, sounded the full depths of self-revelation and deliverance. It is for this reason, therefore, that we are safest if, even in language, we keep close to the categories and symbols used by Paul in these matters.

What, therefore, could only be taught with difficulty to the men of old through the hard knocks of life, is made absolutely plain to us in the Scriptures. We see what sin is, what the flesh is, where it dwells in us, and how we can be delivered. We are in the position of a traveller who has sign-posts along the road, in contrast to the pioneer who has to hack his way through virgin forest.

After we have recognized, therefore, the old man, "the sin that dwelleth in me", the ego that needs crucifying, the flesh that lusts against the Spirit, and numerous other Pauline definitions, without further ado the desire for a full deliverance can be expressed and the choice of a total renunciation made. But, it may be asked, "Surely there is a difference between the mere head knowledge of a truth in Scripture such as we may have, and a heart experience such as these men of old had?" Was not the point with the men of the Bible that they were brought to know themselves, by the only way in which we can know ourselves, by coming to grips with life? True enough. That will follow. But they had to grope their way and be delivered by special revelations. For us, rich provision is made. Let us make the most of it. Let us get all the truth we can, absorb it, understand it, soak in such teaching as we find in Romans 6 to 8, following on to Romans 1 to 5, then obey it as far as we have light. We can at least give all that we know of ourselves to all that we know of God.

Having now seen our true enemy, our fallen ego; having traced him to his lair, through sins, through world attachments, right down to our own hearts; according to the measure in which we have truly felt this "sin that dwelleth in me", made fully bare to us in Romans 7, we cry with the Apostle, "O wretched man that I am, who shall deliver me from the body of this death?"

But first we must ask: What is the deliverance I expect? Just this: I have a puny, poisoned, localized self, shut up to its mean "my" and "mine", lusting and having not, desiring to have and unable to obtain. It is alive in me in place of a God-expanded, God-indwelt self which can know all things, have all things, do all things

It is the flesh of which Paul so often speaks, the old man, the carnal nature. Yet it is the very same self that came from the hands of my Creator—the same self, but seduced from its proper function as the hidden and willing servant of the Spirit in the kingdom of light, and taken captive by sin and Satan to be his agent in the kingdom of darkness. It is not something which was created evil and for which the only remedy is destruction or eradication. Such is an impossibility. The God-made self, a ray from His own self, is no more capable of dissolution or extinction than is God's own self. Rather, it is man's ego which has become enslaved, defiled, bedevilled, and must be released, cleansed and restored to its rightful Owner. It may be likened to the man "which had devils long time, and ware no clothes", who was later seen, "the devils departed out of him, sitting at the feet of Jesus, clothed and in his right mind". The same man in two totally different relations, first to devils, then to Jesus.

The important point of this truth, which is missed by many who remain confused as to exactly what the old nature is and what becomes of it, is to grasp that the new man in Christ is basically the same person, same self, same entity as the old man; formerly carnal, sold under sin; now spiritual, sold under holiness. The flesh (I, carnal) becomes the new man in Christ (I, spiritual). It is the Dr. Jekyll and Mr. Hyde of Stevenson's creation, the one becoming the other by an imagined process of metamorphosis.[1]

[1] Paget Wilkes, in his little book *Sanctification*, has an illuminating footnote on this point (page 42): "Many people have supposed and indeed taught that the 'flesh' in its ethical sense as employed by St. Paul is identical with 'the sin that dwelleth in me'—that 'infection of nature

We see it most clearly when we are told to reckon ourselves dead indeed unto sin, but alive unto God through our Lord Jesus Christ. The self is seen here to be the living centre both of the old man and of the new. I am to reckon the self that was once the old man as now dead unto sin, in other words immune from the power of sin as sharing the death of Christ; and that same self now as the new man, alive unto God as sharing in the quickening life of the risen Christ: and we are then told to yield our *selves* unto God as those that are alive from the dead.

Perhaps the best word to describe the process is transmutation (from the Latin *transmutare*, to change). It is a chemical term used by the old alchemists whose aim was to transmute lead into gold, so to change its character that the elements which constituted the lead should be-

that doth still remain in the regenerate'. This has led to endless confusion of thought and misunderstanding, causing divisions where there need have been none.... The flesh *in itself* is not sinful; we are not told to clean ourselves from the flesh but from 'all filthiness of the flesh'. It is 'the *mind* of the flesh' that is 'enmity against God'. St. Paul, in speaking of the '*fruit* of the Spirit', when he talks of 'the flesh', in the very same passage, is careful to say that adultery, fornication, etc., are 'the *works* of the flesh' and not its fruit. They are the '*fruit*' of Indwelling Sin, though '*worked*' out by the flesh; or, to use the language of Col. 3: 5, they are the members of the 'old man'.

"Thayer, the great Lexicographer, describes it thus: 'The flesh in its ethical sense denotes mere human nature, the earthly nature of man apart from Divine influence.' Martin Luther says: 'Thou must not understand flesh as though that only were flesh which is connected with unchastity, but St. Paul uses "flesh" of the whole man—body, soul and spirit, reason and all his faculties included.'

"Now our 'human nature'—'our reason and all other faculties included'—are God-made and God-given, and cannot therefore *in themselves* be sinful. The flesh seems to include our natural appetites, our heredity, our temperament, our environment and upbringing: all God-given and God-appointed. They are the avenues of temptation, and are come the elements which constitute gold, a like process to that which actually now takes place in the transmutation of the atom. And this is the only possible aim of redemption, that the leadened nature of man in the dominion of the flesh should be transmuted into the golden nature of man in the dominion of the Spirit.

If that is the deliverance, who is the deliverer and how does he do it? "Who shall deliver me?" cries Paul. The glory of the Gospel is the answering cry of Romans 8 : 2, "He *hath* delivered"; not "He shall", but "He hath". We are back again to our old theme: all grace, as all nature, consists in the givingness of God. He *has* given rain and sun and food and aid and life to all his creatures; they have but to enjoy them. He *has* given forgiveness, life, adoption, redemption in Jesus, to as many as receive Him: all they have to do is to hear and believe. Aye, and more: He

only sinful when and because they are indwelt and poisoned and dominated by Indwelling Sin.

"St. Paul thus described the flesh in his Philippian letter (3: 3-6). 'I also might have confidence in the flesh. Circumcized the eighth day ... of the stock of Israel ... of the tribe of Benjamin, an Hebrew of the Hebrews', etc., etc. Now none of these things were sinful; they were merely part of the natural man and his upbringing, and yet St. Paul designates them as 'the flesh'.

"St. Paul tells us plainly that the crucifying of the flesh is something *we* have to do—*our* business (Gal. 5: 24). The crucifying of the Old Man on the other hand and the destruction of sin in my members is the work of Christ and Christ alone; it has been done by Christ in His sacrificial death and is wrought out in us by the Holy Ghost. In this we had no hand; we had no power to deal with these terrible foes. If what I have here written is true, it is possible even after we have been delivered from 'Indwelling Sin' to walk and work for Christ in the energy of the flesh. Hence our need to 'die daily', to 'watch' and 'to keep under our body' lest we too may fall and be a 'cast-away'."

has given deliverance from the power of indwelling sin— the law of the Spirit of life in Christ Jesus which *has* set us free from the law of sin and death.

Chapter Eight

FROM ELEMENTARY TO ADVANCED FAITH

WE must examine this matter more closely. We are beginning now to touch on a subject which has caused divisions in the Church. We must face it carefully and squarely, this subject of sanctification, holiness, the victorious life, the fullness of the Spirit, or whatever name we call it. Names apart, it will for ever be a subject of life and death interest to the re-born soul, for his heart hears the summons of his Lord: "Be ye perfect as your Heavenly Father is perfect"; "Be ye holy for I am holy"; and gives its eager assent.

The Holy Spirit has traced the course of the believer's progress along one highway. It is unmistakable. It is Christ. "As ye have therefore received Christ Jesus the Lord, so walk ye in Him, rooted and built up in Him." Where it is a question of the sinner's justification, it is Christ who "was delivered for our offences and raised again for our justification". And when it is a question of the deliverance from indwelling sin, from the fallen ego, once again he points to Christ crucified and risen; but this time in a newer, profounder aspect, nothing like so easily grasped as the simpler fact that Christ died for us.

Romans, Galatians, 2 Corinthians, Ephesians, Colossians, all make it plain. They show that when Christ died and rose again as the sinner's Substitute and Representative, He did so in a complete way. That is to say, He not merely "bore our *sins* in His own body on the tree", took upon Himself their reality, their defilement and their consequences, burying them with Himself in the tomb, and by

49

His resurrection declaring that the sacrifice was accepted and the sinner justified; but also "He was made *sin* for us", He became the sinner Himself as his complete Substitute; sin's fruit as well as root was taken by Him. All that sin had done in man, its indwelling presence in Him, its dominion over Him, its infection of His very self, His ego, He was made all that for us, for man's greatest sin is himself! And when Christ was crucified, sinful man, as well as man's sins, was crucified in Him; when Christ was buried, sinful man was buried in Him; when Christ rose, man rose in Him, no longer sinful, however, but to walk in newness of life.

Perhaps that takes some thought for those who have not yet grasped its implications. Let such study particularly Romans 6:1–13; Galatians 2: 20, 5: 16–25, 6:14; 2 Corinthians 4:10-12, 5: 14-21; Ephesians 2: 4-7; Colossians 2: 10-12, 20; 3: 1-11; 1 Peter 2: 24; and the truth will be made clear.

We look, then, not to the future for something that *will* happen to deliver us, but to the past for something that *has* happened; exactly the same as the sinner sees, not some future hope of forgiveness through some future act of God's grace, but the past historic fact of the Sinbearer on the Cross. He sees; he believes; it is done; he has peace with God through our Lord Jesus Christ.

So now the Christian, longing to be free from the sin and self that binds him, is bidden, not to ask and hope for deliverance in the future, but to look back at that very same scene, at that same Christ crucified, and view Him from a different standpoint. There he is to see himself with and in Christ. He is to say with Paul: "I have been and still am crucified (Greek perfect tense) with Christ; nevertheless I live; yet not I, but Christ liveth in me." He is to do what Paul said: "Knowing this, that our old man is crucified with Him, that the body of sin might be destroyed ... reckon ye yourselves to be dead indeed unto sin, but alive unto God through Jesus Christ our Lord."

He is to see himself crucified and buried with Christ, leaving there in the tomb that flesh, that body of sin; and himself risen with Christ, a new man in Christ, and Christ in him, no longer he that lives but Christ that lives in him.

Ah, now the battle is joined. Now we get back to where we were when last discussing faith.[1] Now we begin to see that present tense faith is much more difficult than past and future believing. For we find that, though we may believe with ease that the past is forgiven and the future assured, by no means so easily do we truly believe, still less be fully assured, that the present fact is true; that our old man *is* crucified with Him, and that we *are* risen with Him, set free to seek those things that are above. Such a believing simply comes in direct conflict with realities as we know them about ourselves. It simply is not true.

And this brings us face to face, where we have not got yet, with the root and marrow of faith. It also brings us up again to that question we previously raised: Is theoretical knowledge enough? Can we get through with a head knowledge when these men of old had to wrestle on to reach their place of rest in God through storm and wind and tide? No, we cannot. And as soon as we move on from a mere acquiescence in these truths to an honest personal application by faith, the storms begin to blow about us also. We become more conscious than ever of that evil present with us, we feel more than ever the impossibility of our honesty in saying and feeling and knowing with Paul that we are crucified with Christ, and that

[1] Page 25.

He now lives in us. We feel that a statement of faith to this effect is really a hollow sham.

There is a reason for all this. We saw at the beginning that there are two stages of faith—elementary and advanced. We instanced Madame Curie and the discovery of radium as an example of advanced faith on a natural level. We are now reaching the fringe of advanced faith in the spiritual realm. It is definitely more difficult. It reaches into things which are when they appear not to be. It is covered by Jesus' word: "Judge not by appearances, but judge righteous judgment" (i.e. according to what is really so). We see in the manifestation of Himself that God made to Abraham when He was summoning him to that first great act of faith. God revealed Himself as the One who "calleth the things that be not as though they were". It involves, as with Madame Curie in the realm of the natural, having eyes that surely penetrate the realm of the invisible, and a heart that can surely reckon on what is seen there, although it is directly contrary to outward appearances. It takes us to the Word which says that the visible was made out of the invisible, as Moffat translates Hebrews 11: 2.

The swaying battle of present-tense faith is well seen in the instance of Peter walking on the water. Peter was the pioneer in faith amongst the disciples, and it is interesting to watch his development. It was Christ who first lifted the veil and showed him the undreamed of possibilities of faith, and enticed him to make a trial, when He told him to launch into the deep and let down his nets for a draught, after a night without a catch. We see the momentary struggle of faith then, when he weighed up which he believed most, his opinion as an experienced fisherman and that of his brother fishermen on the beach, or the word of this Wonder-worker. He hesitated, then plunged: "Master, we have toiled all the night, and have taken nothing"—that was faith in appearances: "Nevertheless, at Thy Word I will let down the net"—that was faith in the invisible, in the power of His word and the resources at His command. It was a cheese-paring faith, even then, for he let down one net when Jesus had said "nets", and paid for his niggardliness by getting it broken! No wonder he fell at His feet, cut to the quick by his own unbelief.

But he had learned a great lesson. There are resources in God which counteract nature, and man can use them. Next time, Peter needed no invitation. To that figure walking on the water, he calls out, "Lord, bid me come to Thee on the water." No altruistic motive in this, no service for mankind, just a "stunt", we may say; but here Christ had found a pioneer in things of the Spirit and He welcomed the sign. "Come," He said. Peter got out and walked. For the one and only time in recorded history the laws of gravity which govern the sinking of a body in water were counteracted by a higher power for a mere man. How? By Peter's transferred faith. By nature, he believed and acted all his life on the known fact that a man sinks in water. In Christ he saw a higher power operative, enabling him to transcend this law of nature and walk on water. He knew by previous experience that the power of Jesus was at his diciples' disposal. So, deliberately he transferred his faith from its life-anchorage in natural law to that which he could not see or touch, to a power which was upholding his Master and could uphold him.

But he was just a beginner, an experimenter. Along came a big wave. It would engulf him! Away, almost automatically came his faith from its new anchorage back to the old, to the familiar "fact" that we sink in water. And down he sank. According to his faith, so it was. No,

not quite. The hand of the Saviour held him. He had a
ducking for his daring, but he also had gained something
more priceless than any of his more cautious stay-in-the-
boat brethren; an experimental knowledge of the fact that
a man can stretch out the hand of faith, almost at his
whim, and take hold of the hidden power of God.

That he had thoroughly grasped this amazing truth in
the only way truth can be known—by trying it out and
coming some bumps in the process—we see a short while
after. We see Peter, with John, at the Gate of the Temple
called Beautiful. Peter, knowing his secret possessions,
sees a man in need, the lame beggar. Something in his
appeal for alms strikes Peter, something which comes to
his heart as a call to action. "Silver and gold have I none;
but such as I have, give I thee." What has Peter? All the
power of heaven and earth which is released by the Name
of Jesus. The power which he was invited to use in the
fishing incident, which he asked if he might use in the
storm incident, he now knows to be his in Christ, and he
just uses it as his own in his healing incident. Faith has
found its resting-place, the doors of its treasure-house lie
wide open to it: "Such as I *have, give* I thee." And when,
later, he is called upon to explain this miracle of healing,
note where he lays the emphasis: he points them full-faced
to the Christ they have rejected. His is the power. But
note. He does not just say that the Name of Jesus has done
this: but "His name through *faith* in His Name ... yea,
the *faith* which is by Him hath given him this perfect
soundness." Not just the Name, but the applied Name.
There lay Peter's well-learned secret.

Chapter Nine

THE SWAYING BATTLE OF FAITH

APPLY now the secret that Peter had learned to our subject—sanctification by faith,[1] the purifying of the heart by faith,[2] crucifixion, burial and resurrection, with Christ by faith,[3] Christ dwelling in hearts by faith.[4] We face a given set of statements of fact in Christ, pronounced as such by the authority of Scripture; yet they go against appearances, against our feelings, against the consciousness of sin and self in us, against the facts of our many failures in thought and conduct. We are faced, then, with two sets of realities: things as they are in the visible, and things as they are in the invisible, in Christ. Have we not, then, to carry out in the simplest fashion these straightforward laws of faith which we have been examining? We must coolly, deliberately, definitely transfer our faith from the lower set of realities, things visible to us in our inner lives and outer conduct, and place it in God's spoken word: "Ye are dead and your life is hid with Christ in God." We must do exactly as Peter did, when he said: "We have toiled all the night and have taken nothing, nevertheless at Thy word I will let down the net." We must do it. Faith is inner action. We must not flutter around, and hope, and hesitate, and pray. We must *do* it, as definitely as Peter launched out with his net in the presence of his doubtless sniggering fisherman friends; as definitely as he later got out of the boat on to the water. We must make a transaction of faith, maybe on our knees, maybe by

[1] Acts 26: 18. [2] Acts 15: 9. [3] Col. 2: 12. [4] Eph.. 3: 17.

signing name and date against a verse, maybe by public confession or to a friend.

But that is only where the battle of present-tense faith begins. What are we to do with that undertow of unbelief which seems to pull us backward, as when a swimmer struggles against an undercurrent? We must note the following carefully, for it is a point we have not touched on before. There are stages in faith; and we often get into much confusion by attempting to claim as 100 per cent faith what is really only 50 per cent or 25 per cent. In the language of Scripture, there is little faith, great faith, and perfect faith.

Let us examine this more closely. We have said from the beginning that the God-given faculty of faith is the means by which human beings receive and use all God's varied gifts. In other words, faith is not to be confused with mere mental assent to a proposition; that may be called "belief", for want of a better word, although belief in Scripture is usually synonymous with faith. Nor is faith some vague hope for the future. Faith is action; the whole man in action, spiritual, mental, physical. We have abundantly illustrated that by such natural acts as eating and drinking, or the first great act of the awakened spirit in receiving Christ as Saviour. Now, because it is action, it has certainty, and not doubt, as its motivating power. That is to say, we perform the act of eating because we are sure of the food; we see it with our eye, we believe it is good for us. We take the step of humbly accepting Christ, because we are sure of His grace, we believe He died for our sins, we see the statements of Scripture. Faith therefore always *has* the thing in its grasp or at its disposal that it acts upon or uses. That is faith; the having and using the unlimited resources of God in nature and grace. That is perfect faith.

Now, whereas in the simple things of life such perfect faith is ours without difficulty (we see them with the naked eye; the flower we pick, the food we eat, the road we tread upon; and, automatically, we have and use them); it is not so in the things less easily seen or obtainable, as we have already pointed out, whether when delving into the deepest secrets of nature, as does the scientist, or leaping across the gulf into the kingdom of the Spirit reopened to us in Christ. Here we may start with imperfect faith, that is to say, we are not so certain of our facts, our premises; they may often be contrary to what we see with the naked eye, or thought we had learned from life around us. There is an element of struggle in our faith, twinges of doubt, a sense of unreality. Our faith cannot genuinely be said to "have" the thing it would reckon on, but rather to be trying to grasp and maintain it against opposition. There is a labouring faith and there is a resting faith. What Jesus called little faith,[1] for instance, was the action of the disciples in the storm, when He lay asleep on a pillow in the boat and they awoke Him, crying out: "Master, carest Thou not that we perish?" The disciples believed that He could save them, but doubted if He wanted to! There was faith, but of a very watery consistency.

Great faith[2] was what Jesus called the attitude of the centurion, for he not only believed that Christ's word was with saving power, but that He would speak if asked to. He believed Christ could and would. But perfect faith[3] is the description given of Abraham's sacrifice of Isaac. There it is seen that, when God told Abraham to go and offer his only son as a burnt-offering upon one of the mountains of Moriah, Abraham obeyed. It is plain that he had full intention of carrying out God's word to the letter, for he not only bound his son and laid him on the

[1] Matt. 8: 10.   [2] Matt. 8: 26.   [3] James 2: 22.

altar, but also raised the knife to plunge it in him; and not till then, in the last split second, did God withhold his hand. Yet, a few hours before, when leaving his servant with the ass at the foot of the mountain, he had said to him: "Abide ye here with the ass; and I and the lad will go yonder and worship, and *come again* to you." And the comment in Hebrews 11 is that, so sure was he of God's promise of seed through Isaac, that he knew if he slew him at God's word, God would raise him up again. In other words the faith of Abraham always *had* his son, and never let him go. God not only could and would, but could, and would, and had. It was all settled before he started out. He and the lad would come back.

Now, the mistake we so often make is to try to pretend to ourselves that the faith that has really received is ours; whereas, in point of fact, we only have the faith that labours to receive. It is not wrong to have the labouring faith; it is a necessary stage in the process of advanced believing, but it is wrong to try to deceive ourselves about the stage we are in.

The best analysis of labouring and resting faith in the Bible is the description given in Romans 4: 16-22 of Abraham's pioneer act of faith. We there see the process exhaustively outlined. We see faith's beginning and foundation in a discovery of the will of God (a subject dealt with in chapters 18 and 19); in this case it was a word from God: "So shall thy seed be"; for faith always comes by hearing, and hearing by the word of God.

The second stage is the counter-attack of the visible—in this case his and Sarah's age and physical condition. This he countered by turning his back on the visible; a deliberately considered act, for "he considered not his own body now dead, neither yet the deadness of Sarah's womb". This is described as being "not weak in faith";

in other words, he did not just lie down under existing circumstances, as we so often do. He rose up and began to take action, negative action at first.

In the third stage, he passes from occupation with things earthly to things heavenly; from the downward to the upward look. "He staggered not at the promise of God through unbelief." Now the muscles of his faith are rapidly gaining strength: he who had refused to be weakened in faith by natural appearances is mightily strengthened in faith by contemplation of the promisis, strengthened to the point that a sheer impossibility does not stagger him.

At the fourth stage, a radical change takes place: the burden and struggle is replaced by a burst of praise "giving glory to God". Now faith is shining out in noontide strength, and is called "strong". God alone, the God of the impossible, fills the vision; worship and praise take the place of strife and travail, for the soul that is occupied with glorifying God cannot at the same time be obsessed with doubts concerning Him.

At last, at the fifth stage, the topmost rung of the ladder of faith is reached: full assurance; "being fully persuaded that what He had promised, He was able also to perform". Now he *knows*, now he *has*; perfect faith has come. The fulfilment is already his in the invisible, and, as day follows night, will be seen in the visible. And the mighty results of a battle of faith fought and won is seen in its fourfold fruit: it pleases God, it moves God to give public honour to the believer; it has its visible answer in the birth of Isaac; and it is an inspiration to the world.

Some have to toil up the ladder of faith, with varying degrees of labour; but we say again, it is not wrong to feel the conflict with doubt, so long as we are honest about it. Indeed, it is only living faith that doubts, for "faith is not the banishing of all difficulties, but their subordination to greater certainties." One of the most candid remarks in this respect was made by the father who brought his demon-possessed child to Jesus. It will be remembered that he said: "If thou canst do anything, have compassion on us"; and Jesus' answer was: "If thou canst believe, all things are possible to him that believeth." Now notice his reply. "Lord, I believe; help thou mine unbelief." In other words, he recognized frankly two counter-currents in him: one believing, one disbelieving. With one half of him, as it were, he said: "Lord, I do believe." But the other half of him was calling out "Impossible"; and, instead of hiding it, he exposed it and cried for deliverance. That is the way through.

We met three young missionaries who never knew by experience the truths of Romans 6 and Galatians 2: 20, until the camouflage was stripped off their faith. In early days they had maintained that to reckon themselves dead, as Paul had said we were to do, was sufficient. Three years later they gave the illuminating account of how, during their stiff struggle with a difficult language, they became increasingly conscious of their spiritual need and ineffectiveness. They decided to set aside a time for heart-searching. Here they were brought to see that what they had called "faith", when they had said that all they need do was "reckon", was really only a camouflage. What they really meant in their hearts was: "We reckon ourselves dead unto sin and alive unto God, but of course it isn't really so." Now, however, they were not going to be content until they had a real living faith, a full assurance that these things are so; they then described how this assurance came. Actually their earlier faith was not a camouflage in the sense that it was unreal or hypocritical. It was an imperfect faith. It was the first stage, in which conscious faith and conscious unbelief are both active; but their mistake had been to pretend to themselves and others that there was no unbelief; and God can never respond to dishonesty.

Chapter Ten

FULL ASSURANCE OF FAITH

How, then, do we scale this ladder of faith, and pass through the various stages from little to perfected believing?

Some years ago we described in a pamphlet the struggles of the soul that goes through with God, and we will repeat here: God says, "Reckon yourselves dead indeed unto sin and alive unto God." But facts are simply against it! We are not dead to the one nor alive to the other. We must stand to the Scriptures, and yet we must also be realists, true to facts! We will find a compromise, a backdoor out! It says "reckon". That means that we are not actually dead, we only reckon ourselves dead, but are not really so. We are crucified with Christ according to our standing in Him, but not according to our actual state on earth! And so, at the critical moment, we nicely elude the real bite of faith, and begin a crazy, wobbly walk with a foot on both levels of reality, the carnal and spiritual: we endeavour to do exactly what Jesus said it was an impossibility to do; to serve two masters, acknowledge the dominion of two lords, the flesh and the Spirit.

No, that will not do. Faith is the utmost simplicity, but because we are distorted and subtle, it is a long road back to the transparency of childhood. Here is what the Scripture calls the fight of faith. The issue is clean-cut. We are summoned to step right off the level of the visible, the natural, carnal, and take the giant leap into the invisible.

Witnesses are piled on us to press us into it. The inward light. The outward Scriptures. The historic fact of Christ. The miracle of changed lives.

Very well, at last we do it. We state to ourselves that we have begun life on a new level of reality—in Christ. We pronounce the new realities to be the new facts of our everyday life. We *are* dead to sin and alive to God in Christ. We *are* crucified with Him and He living in us. We *have* His love, His wisdom, His power. We *are* in a mystical union with the Godhead. We *are* in a new, time-less, spaceless realm; a fourth dimension, where, in the Spirit, we reach everywhere, possess all things, and touch all lives or supply all needs by the law of this invisible kingdom, the law of faith. And in the magnificence, wonder and glory of this new and full livingness, like Paul, we loose our hold on all the paltrinesses and triviali-ties which were once the sum of all life to us, our little bit of earthly dignity, position and reputation, our miser-able scraps of earthly possessions, our little world of friends and relatives, even our tenacious hold on our minute particle of physical life. All these rivulets of the good things of existence are now merged and submerged in the endless sea of the ALL in Christ... not lost.. merely absorbed, as the light of the night lamp in the morning glory of the sun. How can we grasp tight and cling to our petty dignities, our few bits of things, our tiny circle of loved ones, when hands and hearts are brim full with the wealth of the universe, the honour of divine sonship, the whole family in heaven and earth, and we are busied in praising, blessing and dispensing, in place of coveting, grabbing and keeping?

And then, with a roar and a rush, back flood the plain facts of the old reality. What's the use of all this idealism? Stark realism presents us with unmistakable upsurges of the self-life, patent lapses into the flesh, visible situations of need and lack. Back we swing again into the old beliefs, with their satellites of fear, depression, and fruitless struggling against the enemy.

Yet again in the stillness, the outline of things eternal rises before our misty vision, and we climb back, wearily, shamefacedly, but with grim determination, to the highlands of faith. The things that are seen are only temporal, only the roughened, distorted shell of reality, shattered by the hammer blows of Christ's death and resurrection: such bastard claims to reality we now ignore. The things that are not seen are eternal; here is the heart of reality, the unsearchable riches of the I AM, who now says to us, "In Me, YOU ARE." Yes, here we stand, in Him.

And so the fight of faith sways to and fro. But note carefully that there should be no fight at all! We only fight and struggle because we are still in the infancy of faith; still seeing men as trees walking, so far as the full way of God is concerned. A great veil, indeed, is over the eyes of thousands of Christians just at this point, because they are given to understand that Christianity is ever a struggle and strife against inward and outward foes. No. That is the half-way method of the law, provided only as a schoolmaster to lead us to Christ, to teach us the power of sin and weakness of self, and thus stimulate us to the discovery of true deliverance. That is meeting the negative with the negative; opposing the devil's "Thou shalt not do good", with God's "Thou shalt not do evil", with the consequent exhausting tug-of-war and endless alternation between victories and defeats. But the negative is swallowed up by the positive, the evil overcome by the good. By this method, the evil, the visible, the fallen condition, the oppositions of Satan, are disregarded; while all the energies are concentrated on believing, affirming and standing in the victory of Christ. When this is done, the other merely disappears from view. It becomes an unreality to us, a chimera, a dream. We have passed out of the principle of darkness into the principle of light, and these two cannot know each other. The wrestlings against the rulers of the darkness of this world to which Paul refers, are, he distinctly says, not just a negative recognition of and struggle against such forces, but a positive standing in full mental and spiritual occupation with the great positive facts of salvation, the realization of the heavenly armour, the helmet of salvation, sword of the Spirit, shield of faith.[1]

We struggle and labour and fight in faith, because we have not yet discerned between soul and spirit, the hallmark of the mature. We are constantly moved in the human realm by the impact of the visible. We "see" this or that failing or lack. We "feel" depression. We "hear" an unceasing stream of unbelieving talk. All this affects our minds and conditions, and we seem to have pressing down upon us a mountain of oppression, darkness, inability to maintain our grip on the invisible. We struggle, we strive, and the best we can do is dumbly, without feeling or sight, "to cling heaven by the hems": and the worst, which we more often do, is to let faith go for a season. The battle is fierce. The enemy this time is no dead and gone catalogue of past sins: it is a living, pulsing, corrupt nature. Blows are given and taken in an endless hurricane. One moment, flesh puts its foot on the neck of faith and summons it to surrender, the battle seems hopeless, flesh seems to pop up its evil head whenever it pleases. Another moment, faith rears up again from the dust, flings off the flesh, tramples it under foot and

[1] Eph. 6: 10-18.

shouts, "They that are Christ's have crucified the flesh with its affections and lusts." "Cast out the bondwoman and her son."

Then what happens? Who can tell? The contest was unequal from the beginning, despite all appearances. Faith had the trump card all the time, the victory already won by Him who "having spoiled principalities and powers, made a show of them openly, triumphing over them in the Cross". Only one requirement was essential: that faith should endure to the end and not be bluffed into a surrender.

The same principle can be seen on the natural plane, in the exercise of natural faith. Take as an example the learning of a foreign language. You are faced with a series of hieroglyphics in a book, you hear a medley of sounds around, which mean absolutely nothing. Yet you know that it is a language which can be learned. More than that, you have gone there to learn it. Now that is the first rung of the ladder of faith. However weakly or waveringly, in your heart (even though out of modesty you might not even confess it yourself) you do believe that you can and will get it. Otherwise, obviously you wouldn't try to learn it. So you plod on. Many a time faith and courage fail, the mind is weary and the heart heavy, and you almost give up. But not quite. To give up is faith's unforgivable sin. On you go at it. Months pass. It seems largely to go in at one ear and out of the other. Then—the length of time depends on the difficulty of the language and the ability and industry of the pupil of course—a miracle seems to happen. The day or period comes when, without your hardly realizing it, what you are seeking has found you; what you are trying to grasp has grasped you! You just begin automatically to speak the language, to think it, to hear it. What was an incomprehensible jumble of sounds without, has become an ordered language within the mind. That is the way of faith. It takes what God gives —here a language. It believes that it can attain it. It works at it both by maintaining faith (keeping the spirit up as we call it), and by industry; then the day comes when through faith and through work, the Giver of all knowledge is able to implant in that mind, as part of its very own possessions, that department of knowledge He had already given and it was seeking. Faith has gained the objective God was offering it.

So, in the spiritual fight of faith, the moment or period comes when we *know*. Every vestige of strain and labour has gone. Indeed, faith, as such, is not felt or recognized any more. The channel is lost sight of in the abundance of the supply. As we came to know that we were children of God by an inner certainty, a witness of the Spirit in our spirits, so now we come to know that the old "I" is crucified with Christ; the new "I" has Christ as its permanent life, spirit with Spirit have been fused into one, the branch grafted into the vine, the member joined to the body; and the problem of abiding becomes as natural as breathing.

The way He reveals Himself, and the time, is nothing to do with us. That is where many make their mistake. Faith is not looking for a future revelation, it is realizing a present fact. Faith slips from its moorings when it listens to another's experiences and then says to itself: "I suppose God must come to me like that." Usually God comes in the way and at the time that we least expect, so that we know that it is God and not something worked up by our own efforts or imagination. To some, it may be just a gradual settling realization that these things are so; to another, a great and sudden inward assurance; to yet another there may be the accompaniment of an outward manifestation by dream, by vision, by some sign of the Spirit, as in Bible days.

At the same time, it must be stressed that God does always bear witness to the impartation of His grace in Christ. Indeed, salvation would not be salvation unless we knew it; and the same is true of His full salvation. Do we say that a person is really born of God who only hopes that he is accepted, and hopes that he is forgiven, and hopes for eternal life? The whole Scripture attests that he who believes on the Son of God has the witness in Himself. These things are written that we may know that we have eternal life. The whole glory of a present salvation is that we know and rejoice that He is ours. If a seeker is not sure that he is accepted of God, then we take every means of showing him from the Scripture that he may be sure, and we are not at ease until the light breaks upon him, the burden rolls away, and he is able to say with joy: "Whereas I was blind, now I see."

So it is, also, on the deeper level of Christian experience. We think this is often slurred over by Christian teachers. Emphasis is rightly put on knowing we are saved, then on a full surrender, a whole-hearted acknowledgment of Christ as Lord as well as Saviour: and then the seeking Christian is left to understand that the Holy Spirit automatically fills the emptied vessel; that if we consecrate ourselves, He accepts and occupies our hearts as His dwelling-place. But that is nothing like a profound or Scriptural enough presentation of the full way of life in Christ. It most certainly is not the Gospel according to St. Paul. He takes a far more serious view of the indwelling enemy that has to be conquered, and gives a far more thorough account of how the victory is won. He makes it plain that the power of the flesh, the problem of sin in the believer's life, has to be as thoroughly faced, and the way of deliverance as completely found, as the earlier questions of sin and salvation have their full settlement. He himself could give as ringing a testimony to crucifixion with Christ, to his freedom from the old inner enemy, to Christ now living within, as he could to new birth, forgiveness, and justification.

The question has arisen, even to the point of controversy amongst God's people, as to whether such an experience, call it full salvation, or entire sanctification, or the fullness of the Spirit, or what we like, is separate from the experience of regeneration. Is it, as it sometimes called, a second blessing, a second work of grace in the heart?

The Scriptures do not seem to commit themselves on the point. There is no declaration which could be called final. Obviously, if there were, there would be no controversy. What the Bible does do is to make plain that there are two aspects of salvation through Christ: there is that which centres in Christ dying for us, and that which emphasizes Christ living in us. The former is shown to relate to our sins and their eternal consequences, but the latter to the sinful principle within us and its power in our daily lives.

As to whether Christ is ministered to us in our experience in both aspects at once or separately, the Scripture is silent. Technically, of course, the whole work of salvation was completed by Him for us once and for all by the shedding of His Blood, and by His Resurrection and Ascension; and, when we receive Christ, we receive a whole Christ, in all the fullness and in all the aspects of His saving grace. In that sense, those who stress that there are not two separate comings of Christ to the believer, not two separate works He has to do in us, are correct.

But whether the prodigal returning to the Father with

darkened mind can see more than a glimpse of truth at a time is very questionable. Is not all infinite Truth only assimilated by finite creatures in stages? That is why we lay such stress on the faith side of things. Truth is one and indivisible. All is given us once and for all in Christ the Truth. In him dwelleth all the fullness of the Godhead bodily, and we are complete in Him. But faith appropriates infinite Truth in finite segments. As we feel the need and see the supply, so we put out the hand of faith and take, and God gives what we take. According to our faith it is unto us.

Christian history certainly goes to prove that great numbers of God's people, anyhow, have only come to see this second aspect of salvation as a second need in their lives, a second area ravaged by sin which needs the Saviour; and they have felt the necessity of knowing that He has done this second work of sanctification as surely and definitely as they were given to know by the Spirit that He had done the first.

There, then, lies the point that matters—that we should know and glory in the knowledge of a full salvation; of a flesh that is really crucified with its affections and lusts; of a Christ that really dwells within; of an all-sufficiency for all things that enables us to abound unto every good work. And that, as we have spent these pages in pointing out, is the answer of God's grace to the process of present-tense faith.

Chapter Eleven

TWO TESTIMONIES

Two quite recent and unsolicited testimonies have come our way which particularly illustrate the hunger in the hearts of many Christian people for a fuller life than they experience at conversion. They are worth quoting: one from a householder, wife, mother, and active Christian worker; the other from a young minister of a great denomination. The lady writes:

"I sat for seventeen years under a minister mighty in the Scriptures, who has turned many from darkness to light, and under his preaching I myself grew greatly in the knowledge and love of the truth.

"But in his preaching he dwells continually on the doctrine of the believer's two natures. Romans 7 he presents as the experience of the believer all through his life. It is the perpetual struggle of the two natures within. In this chapter the new nature is impotent, the flesh almighty. He pictures the old nature as a caged lion always ready to spring, as a gushing torrent always pressing to overflow. He says that, though provision has been made through the Holy Spirit for victory, nevertheless there will never be a day actually when that lion will not spring and that torrent gush. He cannot conceive of teaching denying the presence within the believer of an old nature, unredeemed and unredeemable, yet which does not necessarily presuppose eradiction and perfectionism.

"The result of this preaching upon me was that I presented myself to the Lord somewhat in this fashion: 'Lord, I yield myself to Thee completely, this worm Jacob—my heart which Thou has cleansed, yet which is deceitful above all things and desperately wicked; my carnal mind, which is at enmity against Thyself; my flesh, in which dwelleth no good thing; my will, which is rebellious and impotent; my body, which is dead because of sin.' And for the succeeding ten years what misery I lived in, off and on! Not infrequently I got on my knees and said: 'Lord, why don't You let me die and take me to heaven before this terrible old nature of mine breaks out again and increases the number of my sins!' And, incidentally, though as best I understood how, I had yielded myself, I never felt that the Lord had received me. The only thing that saved me really was that early in my Christian life my minister had spoken of a line in Moody's Bible: 'This book will keep you from sin, and sin will keep you from this Book', and I made up my mind that sin should not at any rate keep me from the Book; that I would persist in going back to it in spite of sin.

"For years, as I pondered the Scriptures, I caught glimpses of the blessedness of the life 'hid with Christ in God' and of the 'Sabbath rest of the people of God who rested from their own works', but I knew in my experience very little of that blessedness or that rest. And the more I sought them the more I seemed shut up to the life described in Romans 7.

"Then, one day, by a train of circumstances I will not go into, the Lord placed in our home a missionary of a certain mission. It did not take me long to discover that he had something in his Christian experience that I had not. We had comparatively little conversation, but he did say two things which stuck: 'One must get out of oneself', and 'He that is joined to the Lord is one spirit—that's a great verse'. Neither of these remarks did I understand at all, but every now and then I pulled them out of my mind and chewed them over and wondered what in the world he meant.

"Then, in the wondrous sovereignty of God over our lives, one after another of the missionaries of this society came to stay in our home for longer or shorter periods, and about some of these too there was that indefinable something that there had been about the first, which irresistibly drew me. Christians are 'salt'. One of the attributes of salt is to make thirsty. These Christians made me so thirsty for Christ that I got to be in the state of the bride in the Song of Solomon: 'sick from love' of the One I could not lay hold of; though, as old Matthew Henry puts it in his commentary: 'It is better to be sick of love of Christ than at ease of love to the world.'

"The last to come was 'X', and he was here the longest. I bombarded him with questions, to which he usually gave the exasperating answer: 'I don't know.' He was with us over Christmas day, and Christmas night as we sat about the table he let drop that he did not believe in the doctrine of the two natures. It went through me like an electric shock. A young girl who was there and who lives a most triumphant life in Christ, but who had been taught and accepted the doctrine as a matter of course, said easily, when 'X' explained that he thought he had been the old man and was now the new man: 'Oh, I think we are just talking about the same thing under a different terminology.' I mention this because I believe there are many Christians who, not having analytical minds, grasp the truth of identification and escape the bondage into which the doctrine of the two natures plunges those who, like myself, do have analytical minds.

"When 'X' dropped his thunderbolt, I knew at once he was presenting an idea drastically different from that which I had been taught. It tormented me. So when he left, I got my Bible open to Romans 7 and got on my face before the Lord and said: 'Lord, I simply have to know what this means and I don't care what it costs.' For about three months I pored over Romans 6, 7 and 8. I shall never forget the experience. It was the exact spiritual counterpart of physical travail. I would be in terrible labour over some point, perhaps go to sleep pondering it, and get up with a clear understanding and such rest. Only to find another knot, to know the labour again, and again the rest, as it was cleared up. This went on and on. One by one the Holy Spirit loosed the chains and gave me a deeper insight into Romans 7 than I had ever had into any portion of the Word, and the day came when I knew that Christ had been born in me. It meant deliverance out of Romans 7 into 'the glorious liberty of the children of God', that life where the believer, through reckoning himself dead to sin and alive unto God, becomes henceforth 'just a channel, Christ the Power; just a branch, Christ the Vine; just a vessel, Christ the Treasure; just a lamp, Christ the Light; just a cup, Christ the Water.'

"As I trace the Lord's dealing in my life, I can but worship. I went to the Cross at that time and found the Altogether Lovely One. Before that, Christ had been only God to me, and a rather unreasonable God I thought in my secret heart, since He had given me this sinful nature so that I couldn't help sinning, and then expected me to be grateful to Him for saving me, which seemed to me the least He could do and be respected as God. But I met the Man Christ Jesus at the Cross, and learned that either I must die at His hands or He must die at mine, and that He had chosen to die at mine. And as I yielded Him my tears and my faith and my love which He had never had before, He took me to Revelation 12: 10, '*Now* is come the salvation, and the power, and the kingdom of our God, and the authority of His Christ: for the accuser of our brethren is cast down, who accuseth them before our God day and night.' And I knew the horrible truth that it is not for our sins of omission and commission that Satan accuses us before God, but that he mocks Christ for the *unbelief* of those who profess salvation, who nevertheless confess the lordship of Satan in the words of Romans 7: 16, 17; 'I do ... yet no more I ... but Sin which dwelleth in me,' one of whom I had been. I learned that 'sin' was none other than the unholy spirit (Ephesians 2: 2) and that the Greek word here translated 'dwell' means 'to make a house of', and that I had let the unholy spirit make a house of me, whereas it was the right of the Holy Spirit to make a house of me. I learned that the old man was the house of the unholy spirit, and that that house had been destroyed on the Cross; that he had no rights whatever in the new man and was to be cast out (Proverbs 22: 10).

"I believed at first in the death of self, but I see how right the position is there—that there is no such thing as death to self or self dying, but rather that self alive from the dead and offered up, is given back to its owner, even as Isaac, and becomes the servant of the Spirit; that self is absolutely necessary to the purpose of God, for apart from self delivered unto death there can be no manifestation of the life of Christ in our mortal body (2 Corinthians 4: 11).

"I have such a totally different view of salvation that I am not sure that even yet I could put it into words. I believe that if any so much as turn his head in the direction of the Light, Christ will move heaven and earth, if need be, to get the Gospel to that one. I see the urgency of the great commission: not only that those who have never heard might hear, but also that Christ might possess the lives for whom He died, that He might be set free to roam up and down this earth once more, into every corner of it, in the bodies of those He has redeemed. I see the *morality* of faith's being reckoned for righteousness, faith being the agent through which the living seed of righteousness is implanted in the heart to grow and produce experimental righteousness.

"I used to think that the 'flesh' and 'the old nature' were synonymous terms, but the Lord showed me that Eve had the flesh before she sinned and that it was through the lust of the flesh, the lust of the eye, and the pride of life that she was tempted, even as was the Lord Jesus and as we are.

"I also thought that all Christians were overcomers, basing it on 1 John 5: 4. But the Lord showed me that that referred to the world, and was comparable to the deliverance of the Children of Israel from Egypt; whereas we are to overcome Satan, which is comparable to the conflict in the land of Canaan.

"The Lord gave me a very precious lesson on claiming deliverance for others from Acts 9. He showed me that, though Paul was the instrument for revival, Ananias was the key to it; and that, before Paul could be filled with the Spirit, Ananias must be changed from a hard-hearted Christian, doing Satan's work of accusing the sinner, to a Calvary-hearted Christian doing Christ's work of identifying himself with the sinner, manifested by the outward sign of laying on of hands. 'I and the children whom thou hast given me.'"

The young minister writes:

"All my life I have hungered to know God better. I looked in the book of Acts, and the description of the Christians there did not correspond with the lives of the

Christians I saw around me. I looked for an answer. I read books. I went to hear evangelists. I searched and prayed, but all to no avail. I knew the Lord was my personal Saviour by faith, but there was such a hunger and thirst to know Him better, and to be conformed to His image. Others seemed to be warm, but to me the Bible was more or less a dry book. I even tried the world, thinking a thorough conversion from sin might solve the problem. But it did not. My heart was still hungry.

"I don't say that my life was constantly bleak. I experienced periods of joy that were unspeakable, which lasted for months at a time, followed by periods of depression. I graduated from the art department at the University of M., but had no joy in contemplating that career. In 1936 the Lord led me to take up theology. I graduated from theology in 1939, and accepted a call as pastor in northeast M. in that year. I was eager to see souls saved, but the people were not willing, and my preaching dried up. In desperation, an old deacon and I met together daily for prayer and Bible study, and to our surprise we saw things in the Word of God which seemed to upset our childhood teaching. We faced God on the price it would cost, agreeing to pay it. Then in July about four and a half years ago, the Lord revealed to me the wonderful fact of my identification with Jesus in His death and in His life; that it was no longer I that lived, but Christ was now my life.

"My entire life changed. The Bible became a new book. God gave me the gift to lead others into sanctification. He gave me Bible classes. He led hungry souls to me. He opened the radio broadcast for the purpose of making known the life of identification with Christ on the cross, in the grave, in the heavenly places. Hungry hearts have come from everywhere. The group has grown until now

there are three churches in M. who preach entire sanctification. Persecution has resulted. Bitterness has sprung up,
but through it all the joy of the Lord and His grace and
love have been our strength. God has been leading us on
from truth to truth. For some time He has been trying to
teach me the glorious, central key of strength through
weakness. This summer He made it practical in my life
in a very real way, when He showed me that I had no right
to have others right. It was God's right to keep them
wrong until I was right, and that this was true also with
reference to circumstances and temptations. I learned that
I was not to fight them but embrace them, and accept
present circumstances and people and even temptations as
God's most powerful instruments for good. This was one
of the most important revelations of my walk in sanctification."

Chapter Twelve

THE VARIED TEACHINGS OF THE FULLNESS OF THE SPIRIT

DEFINITIONS of this deeper level of Christian experience, as well as the way of apprehending it, have sharply divided the most earnest seekers after Christ's fullness. Some say[1] as we have just pointed out, that the believer has all in Christ at regeneration; there is no second crisis. These then say that there is a gradual growth in Him, coextensive with an enlarging consecration and deepening faith: but that the two natures are always active in the believer, the old and the new, and the motions of the flesh are only counteracted by a sustained walk in the Spirit.

Others[2] agree in the main with this, but go a step further in stressing a second crisis. They say that the believer is born of the Spirit, but also needs to be filled with the Spirit. For this, a further act of total consecration is needed, a presenting of the body to God as a living sacrifice. When this is done, the Holy Spirit automatically takes full possession, and the one who has made this transaction in sincerity of heart can arise from his knees in joyful certainty that Christ now dwells in his heart in

[1] Outstanding exponents of this position are the Brethren: but it is held in the main by the evangelicals of all denominations.

[2] This is often known as "Keswick teaching" and is taught at the hundreds of conventions for the deepening of the spiritual life which are the worldwide offspring of the "Keswick Convention".

all fullness by faith even though he has no special inward assurance of the fact given him: the Christian life is now lived victoriously by the same principle as outlined above, by a continual abiding in Christ which will counteract the varied assaults of the old nature.

Others[1] go further, and it is here that the breach grows manifestly wider. These say that this second work of grace in the heart, this crisis of sanctification, does a definite work in the believer, both negative and positive. Negatively, it purifies the heart, destroys the body of sin, crucifies the flesh, cleanses from all sin. Positively, it fills with the Spirit, perfects love, perfects holiness, sanctifies wholly; all the above being directly Scriptural expressions. Those who preach and believe it testify to the destruction of the old nature, the removal of carnality from the heart, the replacement of the heart of stone by the heart of flesh through the baptism of the Holy Ghost and fire. Yet at the same time, all who teach thus are most careful to stress that such an experience can be lost through disobedience or neglect; that the close walk with God must be maintained; and even that the believer can fall right away from grace and lose his very salvation. Such teaching is usually considered extreme by those who believe in one of the two previous standpoints; it is feared lest those who accept it will claim a kind of sinless perfection,

[1] The "holiness" bodies. It was taught in the early church by the Montanists; by John Wesley and John Fletcher in early Methodism; by General Booth in founding the Salvation Army (who still have their "holiness" meetings, but do not now in a great many cases teach holiness as radically as their founder). The modern denominations who wholeheartedly adopt the "holiness teaching" are the Church of the Nazarene (a large denomination in U.S.A., smaller in Britain); the International Holiness Mission; the Calvary Holiness Church; the Mennonites; the free Methodists, and others.

and thereby throw a cloak of spurious justification over any kind of inconsistent behaviour. That this has been so in Christian history is proved by the warnings of John's first epistle and by examples of extravagance in the Pietistic movements throughout the centuries, but an examination of the present-day movements that stress "entire sanctification", at least such as are known to the writer, show no ground whatever for such fears.

Finally, there are those[1] who maintain the necessity for a second experience and say that, to be genuine, it must be accompanied by the same signs as at Pentecost, as in the centurion's household at Caesarea, and as at Ephesus —the baptism of the Spirit accompanied by speaking in other tongues. The claim to an experience of the fullness of the Spirit unaccompanied by this sign may certainly be a meeting of the seeking soul with God, they say, but cannot be *the* blessing for which the Saviour told the first disciples to tarry at Jerusalem. Indeed, the exponents of this teaching (and they are many, for they claim over ten million converts during the twentieth century), use the "tarrying" meeting as the special season in which seekers

---

[1] The various denominations that go under the general title of "Pentecostal". Some of these are very large. One in U.S.A. has over 2,000 churches; another in Sweden 750 churches, one of them with a membership of 7,000. In England, there are The Assemblies of God (a branch of a much larger denomination in America), Elim Foursquare, The Bible Pattern Church, The Apostolic Church, The Full Gospel Church, etc. Between them these churches also have large representation on the mission fields. It should also be pointed out that not all the Pentecostal people insist on "tongues" as the initial sign of Baptism of the Spirit, although most appear to do so. One of their greatest leaders in England holds that any of the gifts and offices bestowed by the Holy Spirit, amongst those mentioned in Eph. 4 and 1 Cor. 12, is proof of the Spirit's fullness.

cry to God for "the Baptism" and keep seeking until they find. It is very seldom claimed that He "falls on" them in exactly the same manner as at Pentecost and enables any literally to speak in a foreign language, but rather that they speak in an "unknown" tongue, as in 1 Corinthians 14. To speak once thus is the longed-for "sign". To be enabled to speak in an unknown tongue at will is the additional blessing of the gift.[1]

Believers in and users of this "pentecostal" blessing have been practically outlawed from normal evangelical circles. Their claim to salvation is not doubted, but their emphasis on "tongues" is considered extravagant, dangerous, and even by many demoniacal. Extravagant examples are quoted of people supposed to be speaking in tongues, when missionaries present have recognized the language and heard with horror a stream of blasphemies poured forth. Examples are given of people rolling on the floor at tarrying meetings, indeed a nickname sometimes given them is "holy rollers". It is not doubted that there are extravagances, nor is that to be wondered at when particular stress is laid on the emotions and less on the reason, but Christians need badly to learn not to confuse exceptions with rules, and not to elevate the story of a particular lurid incident, which is probably second-hand and apocryphal, into a general standard of behaviour. For the truth is, even while admitting extremes in some

[1] 1 Cor. 12: 10. A note from the Rev. Noel Brooks on this point says: "The word 'unknown' in 1 Cor. 14, is not in the original and is printed in italics in A.V., while R.V. omits it. The tongue, or to use a modern expression, 'language', spoken is not ESSENTIALLY unknown, but may be, and generally is, unknown to the assembly to whom it is addressed. There have been a number of well-authenticated cases amongst modern Pentecostals of the language being understood by persons present."

places, whether ostracized by the generality of believers or no, God's seal is as much or more on "The Pentecostals" in the salvation of souls than on any other denomination of a like size. Nor have they their superiors in generous giving, warmth of fellowship, or liberty in prayer.

What then do we learn from all this? Surely, that it is not a question of one emphasis being wrong and the other right, but that each is given a special angle of the all-embracing truths of the Christian walk and warfare. That is their particular message; it is their calling to stress it and to reveal its eternal values to the whole Church, not to the exclusion of other emphases, but complementary to them, each having its rightful place, each contributing to the other, but all pointing to the one central figure of Christ.

Thus those who maintain that all is ours in Christ in conversion, and that no "second blessing" is needed, have as their particular message the all-sufficiency of Christ. They point to Christ in Himself. They call on the soul to be occupied with Him. They are busied in showing Him forth from every page of Scripture. But their particular danger is so to concentrate on the objective aspect of Christ in all the Scriptures, on His Person and Glory, that they insufficiently stress the necessary response of the believer in separation and consecretion, and his need of the fullness of the Spirit.

Those who teach a "second blessing", the filling of the Spirit after regeneration, in their message given at hundreds of Conventions "for the deepening of the spiritual life", stress consecration as the main prerequisite for this blessing, resulting in separation from the world and dedicated daily living and public witness. The filling of the Spirit, they say, is God's ready response to the act of consecration; therefore the core of their message is the call to a full surrender. Their danger is that, in thus stressing entire consecration as the main doorway to the fullness of Christ, they stimulate a believer to surrender with greater emphasis than they do to faith. But it is faith that sanctifies, even as it is faith that saves. All the repenting in the world is only useful as a preparation for believing; and all the consecration likewise.

The exponents of "holiness teaching", of entire sanctification, centre their attention on heart purification by faith, as a definite experience which gives deliverance from indwelling sin, fills with perfect love, and endues with power to live a holy life and bear an effective witness. To them the mere call to consecration and the receiving of the fullness of the Spirit does not solve the problem, because it does not sufficiently expose and neutralize the hidden foe, the worm at the roots of man's being, the flesh which lusts against the Spirit. Merely to present the body as a holy temple unto the Lord and to count on His indwelling is to turn too much of a blind eye towards the other occupant of that temple, the indwelling sin of Romans 7, and to leave it too ignored and unmolested to reveal its presence in no uncertain way in the daily life: "for when I would do good, evil is present with me". Their message, then, would get to the root of things, lay the finger on the sore spot in man and provide the remedy; the blood which not only gives "remission of sins" (the fruit), but "cleansing from all sin" (the root); the Cross upon which not only did He bear our sins but crucified our affections and lusts; the tomb, where not only was He buried but we with Him. Made free from the law of sin and death, we rise in Christ, purified in heart, perfected in love, alive unto God, yet not we but Christ living in us. And all this by one definite sanctifying experience in response to the "faith of the operation of God"; or as Moffat puts it: "as you believed in the power of God"; a faith which has clear witness borne to it, a faith which both receives and knows, and which enters into rest. Thus this emphasis points not only to consecration but also to faith; to man's receiving rather than to his self-giving faculty; and to God's completely satisfying and sanctifying response of grace given in one moment of time.

Its dangers or weaknesses are a possible over-stress of the negative side of the sanctifying experience; of purification rather than infilling; of death rather than resurrection in Christ; sometimes drawing too much attention introspectively to the believer's inner condition, rather than to his indwelling Saviour, and leading to repression in place of child-like liberty. But, much more serious, and this is the chief objection raised to this form of teaching by its critics, extreme and seemingly illogical and dangerous emphasis, they say, is laid on the elimination of the flesh by the one crisis of entire sanctification; while insufficient explanation is given of how the appearance of sin is to be accounted for in the believer's life after this "death to sin", this "removal of carnality from the heart". The crisis is stressed and explained at the expense of needed teaching concerning the subsequent process of the daily walk in the Spirit. The perfection claimed for the sanctification experience is not always squarely reconciled with the imperfections of the daily life. It is sometimes difficult to get "holiness" teachers even to face up to the apparent illogicality of their position: yet we think that some approach to an adequate explanation can be given, as we will endeavour to show when we examine the question of temptation.[1] But the fact of this apparent discrepancy

1 See Chaps. 13-15.

and the lack of a plain explanation is an undoubted hindrance to many who feel that in other respects this holiness message and teaching is of paramount importance: and it may also produce bondage and questionings, or, worse still, minor hypocrisies and concealments, in the hearts and lives of earnest "holiness" people.

Those who emphasize the baptism of the Holy Ghost "with signs following" give a leading place to the gifts of the Spirit. They teach the believer to seek and expect the same manifestations of the Spirit as in the days of Pentecost, miracles of healings, gifts of tongues, and interpretation of tongues. There are the gifts and there are the fruits of the Spirit, both recorded in Scripture. The fruits are seen in the character and conduct of daily life: love, joy, peace, gentleness, self-control. Some of the gifts[1] have a more supernatural, supernormal appearance; it is not usual nowadays for Christians commonly to speak in tongues, to have powers of healing or prophecy. Yet these gifts were plainly in evidence in the early church, even the Apostle Paul thanking God that he "spoke with tongues more than they all". And it is upon

---

[1] An interesting comment on the relationship between natural ability and the gifts of the spirit, and how the two meet and produce their continued contribution to the glory of God in a redeemed personality, is in William Kelly's *Notes on the Ephesians*, p. 146. He says: "There are these two things, the ability which is the vessel of the gift, and the gift itself which is, under the Lord, the directing energy of the ability. Paul was a most remarkable natural character; but besides this, when called by the grace of God, a gift was put in him that he did not possess before, a capacity in the Holy Ghost of laying hold of truth and of enforcing it on people's souls. God wrought through his natural character, and his manner of utterance, and his particular style of writing; but everything, though flowing through his natural ability, was in the new power of the Holy Ghost communicated to his soul."

a revival of these gifts, especially speaking with tongues, both as evidence of the baptism of the Spirit and as equipment for worship and witness, that stress is laid (although that is not meant to imply that the fruits of the Spirit are not taught and emphasized).

Now, upon closer examination, we find that speaking in tongues is a form of ecstasy. The tongue is no longer under rational control. The emotions are greatly intensified. The conscious mental processes are suspended. Often the body is shaken. Sounds come from the throat in a rhythmic stream which are usually completely unintelligible to the natural ear, yet they find a response in the consciousness of a fellow-recipient of the Spirit, one who has the gift of interpretation of tongues, who is able quietly and sanely to interpret them in intelligible language, "usually in the form of exhortation, sometimes of adoration and praise, and very rarely of prediction". Those who have this gift can exercise or restrain it when and where they will. The spirit of the prophets is subject to the prophets. They also testify to the sense of glory and worship which fills their souls, which is in accordance with the statement of Paul: "He that speaks in an unknown tongue edifies himself." Furthermore, it is to be noted that the baptism of the Holy Ghost accompanied by speaking in tongues is usually only experienced (though there are exceptions) after long and intense seasons of waiting and seeking, crying and groaning before God.

All this goes to show that this experience is preeminently a manifestation of the Spirit through the emotions. It is a presenting of the personality to God with such a complete abandonment and at such a pitch of intensity that the reason is finally transcended, the conscious being submerged, the love of God and the power of the Spirit flooding in through the whole range of the emotions.

In this rational age, however, we are quick—and foolish—to despise and deride emotion. Such an experience as the above appears eiter ridiculous, hunnecessary or excessive. Not so, indeed. For one thing, it was the experience of Pentecost, repeated on the historic occasion when the Gospel was first preached to the Gentiles:[1] it was common in the early church.[2] Paul the rational, the master of logic, thanked God that he spoke with tongues more than they all! For another, the stirring of the emotions is the source of every human activity. No emotion as a driving force, no creative thought; no emotion, no great achievement; no emotion, no deeds of love nor exploits of faith. Love is largely compounded of emotion. God is love.

Therefore, in stressing the baptism of the Holy Ghost with this sign following, the advocates of this teaching are penetrating to the most sensitive, most powerful chord in human nature, and are stirring their hearers to seek and find the living God through that avenue. The result is a people whose joy knows no bounds: fervent in testimony, free in prayer, large in heart, wide in generosity; with the warmth in their message and fellowship which attracts more hearers to their usually humble halls than probably any other denomination of equal size.

But it is also true that such a presentation has its many real dangers. Too often, reason is given practically no place at all: all is emotion. The balance is not kept; joy becomes mere noise, and preaching a string of emotional exclamations. Sometimes the gifts of the Spirit are stressed almost to the exclusion of the fruits, and little taught about holiness and separation.[3] The gift of tongues is not always

1 Acts 10: 44-48.
2 I Cor. 14.
3 In all fairness it should also be remarked that "there are many Pentecostal pastors who do strive to inculcate moral ideals and lift the

controlled and used in the orderly manner enjoined in Scripture, but may be exhibited for selfish enjoyment or fleshly display, sometimes even combined with inconsistent living; for the expansion of the emotional life carries with it the danger of a reaction into sensuality, unless the walk with God is closely maintained. Also demonic possession, in place of the Spirit's baptism, is possible when the being is so completely handed over, if anything less than God Himself through Christ is the genuine objective of the seeking soul.

Thus these four main categories cover the varied avenues by which the people of God "grow up into Him in all things".

Growth, consecration, purification, fire. These four words might sum up the four presentations. Each is obviously included in the measure of the stature of the fullness of Christ. Each is Scriptural and, in some measure, of course, each is taught by all, and all by each. Is not, therefore, a largeness of Christian tolerance called for? In our emphatic finite way we see some aspect of truth; it is a divine revelation to us; it revolutionizes us; it is our message to our generation. To us it seems more important than perhaps any other truth, and more relevant to the needs of our day. The Spirit seals it by blessing it to many other lives. It appears to us, at least with our often parochial and limited view of things, as the message which

general level of spiritual life. As a matter of fact I suppose there is as much *negative* separation amongst the Pentecostal people as amongst the Holiness. The rank and file of the movement not only are total abstainers, non-smokers, etc., but almost entirely deny themselves pictures, theatres, and even musical concerts and novel reading. As one who knows the inside I would say that mere separation is not our need in the movement, but positive development of Christian character."— Note by Rev. Noel Brooks.

has God's special blessing upon it, the word of the Lord for our day. The Bible seems full of it, to whatever passage we turn (for it is a law of life that we always see what we look for; we select and attract to ourselves from the whole sum of things that which holds our particular interest and attraction; a truth the Psalmist touches on when he says: "With the merciful Thou wilt show Thyself merciful; with the upright, upright; with the pure, pure; with the froward, froward.") Just because we are finitely human, we shall most probably overstate our own particular viewpoint, overrate its value in relation to the whole, and underrate other viewpoints. And so we get schisms and splits!

We must be true to what we see. No man can preach another's message. God sends us each out to be ourselves; and, in presenting our convictions, perhaps it is almost impossible for us to see equal truth in somebody else's. Perhaps we are not even meant to, for each is needed to counter-balance the other and to counteract our chronic tendency to overstate and overenthuse. The all-at-conversionist cannot "see" the second-blessing. The-flesh-versus-Spirit teacher cannot accept the entire-sanctificationist. And none of them can agree with the Pentecostal!

But can we not have such a large view of our essential unity in Christ, of the vastly greater fact that we all centre in Him, revere His Word, rely on His Blood, preach His Gospel, that we make more of our unity than of our differences? Can we not fellowship together, meet on common platforms, join in common conferences, and not thereby lose our liberty of free expression? As we state with thankfulness where we agree, so let us also state where we disagree; but let us do it with humility, as well as with conviction, and with good humour. We know that we are of God and the whole world lieth in the wicked one. We are not many, and the whole world is very great. How essential then that we stand together. God gives certain platforms for certain messages. That is right. Let each message be declared without fear or favour. But let there be room also for recognition that there are other godly brethren who cannot see all that we do, but who also probably do see many things that we don't! And let us welcome them too.

Surely this is the unity of the Gospel, a unity that allows an absolute liberty. Compulsory unity, such as in the Church of Rome, is death. We do not believe in these unifications that bind the people of God down to man-made leadership, and man-made laws, or even man-made interpretations of God's Word. A unity based on compromise is equally false and fatal. The fact is that a great deal of the complaint of lack of unity in the Church of Christ is nonsense. They mistake uniformity for unity. There *is* an eternal unity between God's born again people. There *is* a world-wide family of God here and now on the earth. No formal resolutions, no legal gettings-together, are needed. Any servant of God, who travels the world to-day in Christ's Name and unlabelled by any particular denomination which may limit the bounds of his fellowship, does not take long to discover the marvellous reality of God's present-day family. He will go from hut to mansion, from white to black, from lord to labourer. He will have to try to understand nearly every language on earth, and when he cannot, the hand grip and smile of welcome will bear the same family message of love.

This is the living unity without uniformity. Probably it is as far as God wants His people to go. Federations may be possible, or fellowships, if they really give individual freedom for each to express their worship and faith as they wish, the only bond of union being the Scriptural test that Jesus is confessed to be the Son of God who has come in the flesh;[1] but closer union probably only ends again in divisions. For the Spirit *will* be free. He *will* break forth in this direction, if He is bound in that, He is life, not letter; and even the very sacraments of Baptism and Communion ordained by the Saviour and the Apostles can be no standard of union. If they are our focal point, what about those great communities who practise neither? Are they to be excluded? If ordained ministry is to be necessary, what about that world-wide community of believers who consider such a ministry unscriptural? And if some doctrine of the Spirit, what about our "Holiness" and "Pentecostal" brethren?

The truth is that multiplicity of sects is not an evidence of disunity, but of healthy variety.[2] There always will be such and always should be. The Spirit will always be manifesting Himself in some new way; not with a new Gospel, but with a new presentation of it, or new emphasis of some neglected aspect of it, or new application of it to present-day needs. The wise will welcome all; not join all, but recognize in each with joy some fresh outstretching of the saving hand of God to the world. "Wisdom is justified of all her children." Even democracy teaches us that the party system is healthy, and, indeed, the evidence of true liberty and the only means of giving

[1] 1 John 4: 2, 3.

[2] Being in a finite world we only "know in part" and so easily tend to overemphasize what we do know at the expense of other aspects of truth; and, being in a fallen world, we all too quickly stifle the vital spirit of truth by the mere dead letter. Hence the necessary uprise of a new emphasis. The day is coming, the day of the Lord's return, when all such varieties will cease, when "we know even as we are known" and when "we all come in the unity of faith and of the knowledge of the Son of God unto a perfect man".

expression to the all-round views of a people; new parties must arise, as the left-wing parties of our day, to express new political insights and convictions. In the House of Commons a leader of the opposition is even paid a large salary to marshal the assaults of his party upon the viewpoints of those in power!

The sad thing is our engrained tendency to regard all other sects as sheep-stealers and rivals. It is really only the outward expression of our own innate selfishness. If another group comes into a town, with fervour and freshness, with some strong and joyful emphasis on Gospel truth, and some of my congregation leave to join them, why do I object? It is only taking away from me, not from Christ. Let me rather be humbled that others should come, and that there should be a warmth, attraction and power with them which I do not appear to have. If only I truly consult the interests of Christ and of my flock, I will always exhort them to go where they are happiest in Gospel fellowship, and only to remain with me if they find this fellowship most vital.

"Endeavouring to keep the unity of the Spirit in the bond of peace."

Chapter Thirteen

THE CENTRALITY OF THE WILL

MAN's freedom of will[1] is the central point of his creation in the image of God. It is this that makes him a son and not a creature. God has in him his "fellow" with whom He can have "fellowship"; not a relationship of mechanical compulsion, but the loving intercourse of free hearts and minds.

> *Whose plan was to create man and then leave him,*
> *Able, His own Word says, to grieve Him,*
> *But able to glorify Him too,*
> *As a mere machine could never do.*[2]

But freedom involves self-consciousness. It means that its possessor knows himself and his own desires and opinions. He has a self-conscious ego, and the natural, basic instinct of self-conscious being is to please itself. Self-satisfaction, self-preservation, self-propagation, and self-expression are the only possible or conceivable instincts by which life can be preserved. "Love thy neighbour *as thou lovest thyself*", could be an extension of the words of Jesus. "No man ever yet hated his own flesh; but nourisheth and cherisheth it", said Paul. Of God Himself, from whom our nature is derived, it is said: "Thou hast created all things, and for Thy pleasure they are and were created"; and of Christ the Son: "For the

[1] An attempt at examining the origin, meaning and use of trial and temptation in the nature and destiny of man is made in Appendix I.

[2] Browning, *Christmas Eve.*

joy that was set before Him He endured the cross, despising the shame." No natural desires or instincts, therefore, whether of spirit, soul or body, are wrong; but, on the contrary, absolutely right. Not only the natural appetites whose use preserves and propagates life, but also the instincts of pride, anger, ambition, jealousy,[1] just as much as the more usually applauded instincts of love, faith, hope; instances can be found in Scripture where every one of the former are attributed to God and to holy men of God.

But God is love; not self-pleasing but self-giving love. From all eternity He does find His pleasure and satisfaction (in that sense He is self-pleasing), but He finds it in love; love of His Beloved Son, love of His creation, love even of the loveless. If we may reverently say so, God has been from the beginning the Sublimated Self, fulfilling in Himself the word of Jesus to men that he that saves his soul loses it, but he that loses it for Christ's sake finds it. Self-pleasing and self-giving are eternally joined in Him and form one perfect will; "The good pleasure of His will", as Paul calls it.

That which is the eternal condition of the uncreated God has to become the fixed condition of man by an all-embracing choice. That choosing is essential as the only method by which man's powers are stirred to action. In everything there is an alternative, and a tension of choice between these alternatives; and the choice sets the wheels of action in motion along a definite course. I desire to go somewhere, for instance. I go here? Or I go there? Which? I choose. Right, that is settled. Now I am free to go as I desire, with all my energies centred in the one direction. But until that choice is made I am not free. I cannot act. A double-minded man is unstable in all his ways.

So Adam and Eve had to choose. It was in the nature

[1] e.g. 1 Cor. 1: 31; Eph. 4: 26; 2 Cor. 11: 2.

of things. Since they and the race they were to found were destined to carry out a vast programme of human development, the first great basic choice had to be made as self-conscious beings. Would their self-pleasing take the form of lust or love; in other words, of selfishness or self-giving? Would they choose the possible course of pleasing themselves in disregard of others, or of pleasing themselves in the service of others? And the "others" meant, in their case, first of all, their Maker, God. It was man's fundamental choice, implicit in its nature, the choice that decides the destiny of heaven or hell, the choice that fixes him on one road or the other. (Only, since that day, man has lost even the power of making this choice, so vitiated has his nature become, and God in infinite grace has replaced this too-high alternative by one within man's fallen reach, just to accept and believe in a Saviour manifest in the flesh, who cleanses and changes the nature and renews the power to make and maintain the ultimate choice of man's spirit.)

At this point there entered the one who had made that fatal choice before, the first in the universe to do so, the first one to discover that there is an eternal hell for those who choose the way of darkness, as much as an eternal heaven for the children of light—Lucifer, the devil. By subtle display of the attractions of the forbidden fruit, of the tree which symbolized the selfish God-denying choice, the kind of attractions which have since been the corrupting virus of the world: the lust of the flesh (a tree good for food), the lust of the eye (a tree pleasant to the eyes), the pride of life (a tree to be desired to make one wise); by subtle detraction from the goodness and love of God; by these means evil influences were brought to bear on the will of the two, and the fatal choice made.

Since then man's will has been corrupted. He is born

with a bias to lust, to selfishness, to hatred of God. And not only man himself, but the whole of nature has caught the infection. Peter speaks of the corruption that is in the world through lust. John warns of a world and the things in it which are not of the Father. The very animal creation shows the proof of it in tooth and claw and sting. Every touch of man on the world tends to display all that will stimulate lust through the eye, in the flesh, to the mind. The world is a monstrous instrument to temptation.

Renewed in Christ, crucified and risen with Him by faith and inward witness, once again the choice has been fully made by some through the enabling of His Spirit, Who was spurned in that first garden. Our wills have become one with God's. Now God works in us to will and to do of His good pleasure. Our set purpose with purified hearts has become to love Him with all our strength and our neighbour as ourselves. But we remain in a vitiated world. Almost all things around us, sights and sounds and influences, are charged with temptation. Satan remains the prince of this world, the god of this age. Our bodies, still in the bondage of corruption, were in the past given over to sinful habits and respond very often more easily to temptation along the lines in which they were over-indulged. Most people have special sins that "easily beset" them.

Temptation, therefore, remains the constant element in which we live, sometimes consciously, always there subconsciously in the very environment. But we are to understand that this is both our blessing and our battlefield. For it is by conquest over temptation, by the integration and invigoration derived from the struggle, that we both move forward decisively and definitely ourselves along a clear line of action and also release new redemptive forces in the world.

Chapter Fourteen

NOWHERE is the true significance of temptation more clearly seen than in the historic forty days on the mount of temptation. There "see the Christ stand" we might say with Browning. We watch that tremendous scene, the last Adam, the Word made flesh, come to fight and win the battle that the first Adam lost. We see Him with His human instincts, passions and powers, true Man in spirit, soul and body. We watch the battle raging over forty days, the last word that can be spoken on the subject of temptation and its proper meaning and value. We see this Man complete in manhood's powers, forty days "tempted of the devil".

Temptation had started before then, of course. We catch a previous glimpse of it, when by a subtle solicitation through the channel of His enlarged and illumined spirit, the young lad of twelve might have been led away by the devil in disguise to follow the trail of false favour in place of filial obedience to His parents. But now He was a Man in the fullness of His power, and the only Man in history to whom those tremendous words had been or could be spoken, but a few hours before: "Thou art My Beloved Son, in whom I am well pleased."

Consciously anointed by the Holy Ghost, knowing in Himself that the Spirit of the Lord was upon Him to fulfil the greatest commission ever given to man; to be the world's Saviour, to be the Man of Destiny whose Name had been on the inspired lips of sage and prophet since the world began, the longed-for Messiah, there was still one thing needful, a final, irrecoverable choice of free will, a voluntary self-dedication of every power of spirit, soul and body to this one end. And for that the devil was necessary!

As light cannot be seen to shine except in contrast to darkness, nor heat felt to warm except in contrast to cold, so man cannot know his nature fixed Godward except by his refusal to fix it devilward. So Jesus met Satan on that mount. His body had natural instincts. Only through a right use of these instincts could He be preserved fit for its exacting ministry: He must eat, drink, sleep. In the fierceness of the conflict and the choice to be made, He had not eaten food for forty days. He was hungry; and then the suggestion stabbed home to Him: "Your new powers over nature. Use them. Make bread." In a moment the battle was joined. Was His body to be master or servant? Was He to move at its dictates, or was it to move at the dictates of the Spirit who controlled Him? The word was spoken. Not a powerless negative, a mere "No" which leaves the nagging temptation unrelieved; but a triumphant positive that swallows up the negative: "Man lives by every Word of God." That temptation was the highway, the only highway to bodily victory. It "drove" the Saviour to a choice: that Spirit should control body, not body Spirit. It was settled. Henceforth His body was an instrument for God's glory: His appetites were the natural means by which it could be kept in working order.

Soul greater than body, as spirit than soul. In the soul repose all the vast powers of the personality—to think, to will, to feel. All the mighty achievements of man, in art, in science, in literature, in action, flow from the soul. The genius, the leader, the inventor, the discoverer, have all great souls. And none so great as the human Jesus. Satan knew this; for to only one Man has he offered complete world dominion and promised Him the attainment of His objective, showed Him "all the kingdoms of the world in a moment of time"; said to Him "all these will I give Thee". The condition? That he commit Himself into the hands of "the prince of this world" (as He later calls Satan), absorb the spirit that is in the world, and act according to "the wisdom of this world"; for what we worship we assimilate and incarnate. In other words, all the powers of that greatest of human personalities, mental, emotional, volitional, would become the vehicle of world dictatorship, based on the age-old methods of conquest and compulsion, the only technique of government known to man and the spirit that works in man. The alternative? The worship and service of God; and that meant the subordination of these same soul-powers to the ways of His Spirit, to the carrying out of an alternative technique of ultimate world dominion which was in the wildest sense improbable and fantastic, and as totally removed from the way of the natural man as light from darkness. Truth, love, self-giving, meekness, faith, expressed through the concentrated soul-forces of a personality totally given to them, without weapon, without possession, without name, without friend at court, involving even the ignominious death of this "self-styled" king, were to establish a kingdom that would swallow up all other kingdoms and crown Him King of all other kings and Lord of all other lords. What a drama was enacted on that high mountain, worthy of the pen of the greatest of poets. History was in the balance, and that temptation of the human soul was the material from which the plan of the ages took its shape, in which the foundation of the kingdom of God was laid. It was the choice that fixed a destiny; not just His own, but of a multitude which no man can number, of a kingdom that shall never be destroyed.

Yet spirit is deeper than soul. It is the inner ego. It is the essence of a man. It is that which expresses itself through body and soul. It is the "I" which talks about myself. God is a Spirit, and the Father of spirits. It is the spirits of just men made perfect who dwell with Him. It is the centre of my being where God walks and talks with me; His Spirit bearing witness with my spirit, joined unto the Lord, one spirit. And if body and soul must be fixed in God through the stabilizing processes of temptation, so almost must the spirit. Body and soul may be in God's service, yet even in fulfilling His will in our innermost spirit we may still seek to be in the centre of the picture; glory must come to us; people must be drawn to us; our honour and dignity must be upheld; and the impress of the servant, more than of his Lord who sent him, is left on the service rendered. So Satan sought to reach the spirit of the Saviour, when he could not touch body or soul. Let them flock around Him as the miracle worker, as He descends through the air upheld by supernatural power. Let them all see who He is: the Son of God with power. The masses will be at His feet. The ear of the nation will be open to Him. They will be as clay in His hands, to be moulded to His pattern. The alternative? To give Himself to show forth Another as life's final meaning; to point to Another; so that from thought and word and action stands forth the outline, not of the visible Jesus, but of the invisible Father. "He that hath seen me hath seen the Father"; "I have manifested Thy Name unto the men Thou gavest Me ... I have given them the words Thou gavest Me ... and they have known surely that I came out from Thee, and they believe that Thou didst send Me." To worship any flesh, even the flesh of

Jesus, is idolatry. To revere the human Jesus as provider of bread and healer of sicknesses would save no souls, found no new kingdom of the Spirit. To do this, in His flesh, His words, His works, they must see not a man, but God the Spirit, the Word made flesh. And so, on the one hand, He even tried to distract attention from Himself as a miracle worker; on the other, when at last acknowledged by Peter as Son of the Living God, the triumphant cry brust from Him: "Blessed art Thou, Simon, for flesh and blood hath not revealed it unto thee, but My Father which is in Heaven"; adding, as He foresaw through the centuries the world-wide Church which was to be founded on that same principle of inner revelation: "And I say also unto thee, thou art Peter, and upon this rock (a man who has by revelation concerning Christ penetrated through flesh to Spirit) will I build my Church: and the gates of hell shall not prevail against it."

Thus, on the pinnacle of the temple, that final battle of the spirit was fought and won. Satan's weapon of temptation was turned to his own confusion and made the means of confirming the Son as the Servant of the Father. The high road to man's salvation was now opened. The body was not for self-indulgence, nor the soul for self-aggrandizement, nor the spirit for self-exaltation; but the whole Man, Christ Jesus, driven by the Spirit to face Satan's plausible alternatives, by virtue of the very conflict and the choices entailed, came out of that forty days confirmed in His own consciousness and declared before heaven and hell, in spirit, soul and body, to be the Son of God with power, His Father's willing Servant and the world's Saviour. Only once more had such a battle to be fought; shorter, sharper, even fiercer, in three hours of bloody sweat; this time to gather strength by conflict and conquest to be the offering for the sin of the world.

Chapter Fifteen

TEMPTATION ANALYSED

FROM this one perfect insight given us into the meaning and mastery of temptation, we learn several important points. One is that temptations met and mastered are the only high road to stabilization of character and spiritual progress. Temptations always touch the vulnerable point. That is their chief use, as well as their great danger. In a two-way world, laid open to the illegal knowledge and contrasting claims of good and evil, every instinct of body, soul and spirit has to go through the crucible of temptation, and go there again and again, until it can come out purified and fixed in God. We may be sure that every temptation that comes to us comes because it exactly suits our condition, for we are only temptable at the points where we are sensitive to that particular type of appeal. In fact, in one sense we draw our temptations to ourselves. Out of all life's innumerable stimuli which reach out a beckoning hand to us, we automatically select and respond to those with which we have affinity. They draw us. But for every attraction in one direction, in the nature of things there is a counter-attraction in the other. If one is of the flesh, the other is of the Spirit, or vice versa. Thus a choice is forced upon us. We make it. If we know the secret of the Spirit, we do not meet the pull of the carnal with an ineffective "No" (the "thou shalt not" of the law), which leaves the conflict unresolved, or at best gives victory only by the skin of the teeth; but we meet it with the positive, sublimating alternative of the gospel, the "Christ hath delivered us from the curse of the law";

the ringing declaration that the "I" who might respond to the temptation is "crucified with Christ", and now "Christ liveth in me". A victory is won which is real and complete; the draw of the temptation disappears, swallowed up in the greater attraction to the soul of the Living Christ. The instincts of soul or body which were previously divided, part drawn out in affection to the lower and part to the higher, are now all centred and satisfied in Christ. There are none left still to feel the pull of the lower. The temptation has disappeared, not that the stimuli are not still present in the world or the capacity to respond in soul or body not still there, but the counter-attraction of Christ has occupied the whole man. The joy of the Lord is his strength. His choice, stirred into action by the temptation at the point at which his nature was still responsive to that particular temptation, has integrated or reintegrated his nature in God. A further stage forward has been taken in the formation of spiritual character, a further release given for spiritual service, an invisible victory won which undoubtedly has its hidden repercussions through the whole world, and reverberates through eternal history, for "he that ruleth his spirit is better than he that taketh a city". In some instances, in one great contest with temptation, as with Christ on the Mount, a choice of such magnitude and intensity is made that the soul passes completely out of the range of that temptation, and in that matter becomes fully fixed in God. In others, particularly in the lesser temptations of daily living, repeated contests and choices, often interspersed with defeats, form a gradually ascending pathway to habitual victory and ultimate immunity. At the same time, we are clearly warned that many assaults of temptation are our own fault. If we maintained a close walk with God, our hearts would remain so filled and thrilled with His presence that there would be immunity in the moment of assault. "Watch and pray lest ye enter into temptation." Christ wrestled while the disciples slept, and, when the awful moment came, Christ was in calm mastery over His very captors, while the disciples fled. It is right to fear temptation and not meet it, still less welcome it, in a spirit of bravado, lest it overwhelm us with the suddenness of a cloudburst; daily we are to pray: "Lead us not into temptation"; but, at the same time, we can learn and see that temptation is our battleground and opportunity. Such an understanding will give us a healthy, hopeful, not repressed, defeatist or resentful, attitude to life's conflicts.

One other point is of great importance. It is to have a clear insight into the fact that temptation must by no means be confused with sin. In no case is the actual temptation sin, even though at times we have come within its influence through neglect. We have tried to make it clear that all human instincts and capacities are by their nature neutral, neither good nor evil in themselves. The good or evil resides in the heart and will that governs and directs the instincts. Thus, to be drawn by an instinct (whose function is always to respond to stimuli and thus originate action) is natural and normal; whether it be by fear or its substitute faith; anger, or its substitute gentleness; pride, or its substitute praise of another; lust, or its substitute love. It all depends on the choice made. It is at that point that the sin comes in. James, the analyst of human nature, makes this plain.[1] Temptation, he says, comes from an evil source: it is a legacy of the fall. Man is in the environment and atmosphere of this evil thing, proceeding from an evil being, the devil, through his evilly-infected agent, the world. The way temptation works upon us, then, is this, says James: an instinct, a natural desire (called in the

[1] James 1: 13-15.

text a "lust", which can give a wrong impression, for the word "lust" is in the original just a neutral "strong desire", not necessarily evil or good) is stimulated by some object. It "draws" the man and entices him. No wrong in this, except it be the general wrong of a fallen condition which has corrupted man's instincts and made them all too prone to "inordinate affections". But, continues James, the crisis is in the choice; not in the instinct which draws and entices, but in the will of the man who either responds to the temptation or alternatively cleaves to the highest stimulus of an indwelling Christ, and thus lifts his troublesome appetite on to a new spiritual plane of satisfaction in Him. It is here, he says, that sin enters: "When lust hath conceived"; in other words, when man's free will, his power of choice, has been married to the enticing instinct; when he has consented to it, joined himself to it, then the child of that marriage is sin.

This is a liberating thought for many Christians, for many endure much inner condemnation and bondage through constantly feeling that they have guilty desires, and that as a consequence their Christian profession is hypocrisy because their inner condition is a secret contradiction to it. Not so. It is natural for instincts to be the instrument for temptation. The tempter is the evil one. The sin is in the response, not in the instincts; but, alternatively, victory in the temptation fixes those instincts more and more definitely as agents for revealing God to the world. Let us, then, be free and unafraid in Christ, healthily recognizing what is the battleground, what the enemy, what the weapon of victory, and what the outcome.

Chapter Sixteen

FAITH IN THE DAILY LIFE

IT is obvious from an examination of the Bible record, both in the Old and the New Testament, that in the lives of the men of God there was invariably a background of fully-functioning faith, we might almost call it a technique of faith, to all their activities. We say fully-functioning faith, because the simple word faith (together with the other words of Christian experience which have become commonplaces, such as love) has been so watered down from its original content that to many it now conveys very little more than merely its first stage—the belief that God *can,* not necessarily that He *will,* and still less that He *does.* But fully-functioning faith includes all these.

We do not think that we can stress a more important subject to all active Christians than this fully-functioning faith. Our Scriptural grounds for doing so are obvious. It is made as plain as daylight that the right and full use of faith is the mainspring of every spiritual achievement. Pre-eminently this is so, of course, in the attaining of spiritual objectives, in the salvation of souls, in revival, in all concerns of the Church of Christ. But by no means exclusively so. Faith is shown to be the principle of effective action, of supply, of the solution of all problems, in every single thing, small or great, temporal and material, in the home or in the business, at work or at play, that affects a Christian's daily life. It is necessary to say this, because many people have got the idea that victories, deliverances, or the supply of need by faith, are privileges confined to those set apart for the Christian ministry, and not to be experienced in the ordinary home and the every-day life.

Watch the men of the Bible and it will be seen how central faith is in all their actions and attitudes. That unique chapter, Hebrews 11, the only approximation in the whole Bible to a biographical outline of Bible characters, clinches the matter for us. It is written for the one purpose of showing that faith was the dynamic of all they did. Abraham's whole life centred round obtaining the heir through whom was to come the promised race, and the birth of that son was simply and solely an achievement of faith. Moses, in leading the revolt against the Egyptian oppressor, was but a straw fighting against a mill race until he learned the secrets of faith: from then on, the position became exactly reversed; the weak, the base, the foolish, put to confusion and utter rout the wise, the mighty and the noble. Not only that, but, just as simply, the ordinary necessities of life, food and drink and protection, were obtained by faith for two millions for forty years in a "waste and howling wilderness".

Joshua could lead a successful invasion against seven nations and thirty-two kings, where, before he had learned the secret, one nation nearly overwhelmed him, had it not been on that occasion that Moses knew and used that same secret on his behalf.[1] David learned it as a lad guarding his father's flock; and, by the application of it at a moment of national crisis, though still in his teens, met and overthrew the giant who had scared all the rest of Israel out of their wits. In spite of that, because he did not yet know it as a working principle for all life, as we have previously pointed out, he had to spend eight years as a fugitive in a cave. How well Elijah and Elisha knew the secret and could apply it to an endless variety of

[1] Exod. 17: 8-13.

needs and circumstances. And pre-eminently, of course, the Saviour, who lived in the calm elevation of an inner union with the Father which caused Him to speak of Himself as "in heaven"[1] when on earth, and to act with all the authority and resources of the Creator in human flesh: yet it is equally remarkable and significant that He made it perfectly plain that He knew the secret of union with the Father and the consequent power at His disposal, not through reliance upon the fact that He was by nature the Son of God, but because, as Son of Man, He walked with unfaltering footsteps along the highway of faith.[2]

Not only that, but nothing could be more remarkable than His constant efforts to stimulate faith in His disciples and to impress upon them its working principles. It was to faith that He attributed His "mighty works"; not His faith, but that of the suppliants. To the centurion who asked Him not to come to his house but just to speak the word, He said: "I have not found so great faith, no, not in Israel." To the woman who touched the hem of His garment: "Daughter, go in peace, thy faith hath made thee whole." When the four men let their paralysed friend through the roof, Jesus pardoned and healed him, "when He saw their faith". To blind Bartimeus it was: "What wilt thou that I shall do unto thee?" And then, "Go thy way. Thy faith hath made thee whole." By the Syrophenician woman He allowed Himself to be compelled into action with the comment, "O woman, great is thy faith: be it unto thee even as thou wilt." Others He stirred into faith. He asked the two blind men: "Believe ye that I am able to do this?" To Jairus, when the servants came to say that his daugther was dead, He said: "Fear not, only believe." He told the father of the lunatic son: "If thou canst believe, all things are possible to him that be-

[1] John 3: 13.   [2] e.g. John 5: 19, 20; 14: 10-12.

lieveth"; and afterwards told the disciples that they had failed to cure the boy because of their unbelief. And sometimes it was a rebuke, or amazement at their slowness to believe. On the stormy waters of the lake, after He had silenced the tempest, it was: "O ye of little faith"; and "How is it that ye have no faith?" To Peter it was the same: "O thou of little faith, wherefore didst thou doubt?" And to Martha at Lazarus's tomb: "Said I not unto thee, that, if thou wouldest believe, thou shouldest see the glory of God?" In one case, at Nazareth, it was openly stated that unbelief cut the life-line of power, and "He could do no mighty work there because of their unbelief."

Could any list give clearer proof that Jesus was turning the world's attention to a key that is actually in man's hands, which can unlock at will the storehouses of God's power?

After Pentecost, in the new-born Church, it was obvious that faith was given a pre-eminent place. There were the outstanding incidents of the record in Acts. The lame man healed "through faith in His Name"; the word of faith which brought death to Ananias and blindness to Elymas; Stephen, who, "full of faith and power, did great wonders and miracles among the people"; the command of faith which healed Æneas and raised up Tabitha; the cripple at Lystra who Paul perceived had faith to be healed; the raising of Eutychus; and Paul's statement in the great storm that all would be rescued, adding: "Wherefore, sirs, be of good cheer; for I believe God that it shall be even as it was told me."

To this long list is to be added the complete exposition of "the law of faith" in all its aspects in the writings of all four apostles, Paul, Peter, John and James; the faith that saves, in Romans; the faith that frees, in Galatians; the faith that is tested, in Peter; the faith that overcomes, in

John; the faith that works, in James; the faith that endures and achieves, in Hebrews; the faith that sanctifies, in Thessalonians: the faith that is to be fought for, in Timothy; the faith that centres in Christ, in Ephesians and Colossians.

Chapter Seventeen

Now all these varied examples of faith from both Old and New Testaments, including a great number more not mentioned, have one focal point. If the process of faith be likened to climbing a mountain (although it is not too good an illustration), then the summit is the same in every single case. To understand the route, reach the top and enjoy the view from it, is to practise living faith. So many on so many occasions stop breathless half-way. They just do not get there. Now the summit is the *word* of faith.

Look back again on these incidents in the lives of the men of faith. "Abide ye here with the ass; and I and the lad will go yonder and worship, and come again to you", said Abraham to his servant; it was settled in his heart that God would either provide a substitute sacrifice or raise Isaac from the dead. "Stand still, and see the salvation of the Lord... for the Egyptians whom ye have seen to-day, ye shall see them again no more for ever", said Moses to the terrified Israelites before the Red Sea and with no visible way of escape. "At even ye shall eat flesh, and in the morning ye shall be filled with bread", said he again to them in the wilderness; and these are only two examples of the word of faith which he was constantly declaring. "Shout, for the Lord hath given you the city", said Joshua, before the walls of Jericho had fallen; and a few days previously: "Prepare you victuals, for within three days ye shall pass over this Jordan." "Arise, for the Lord hath delivered into your hand the host of Midian", said Gideon to his three hundred, when facing an army "like grasshoppers for multitude". "Come up after me: for the Lord hath delivered them into the hand of Israel", said Jonathan to his armour-bearer, when the two of them were going up alone against the Philistines. "This day will the Lord deliver thee into my hand; and I will smite thee", was David's word to the giant. Elijah was strongest of them all: "As the Lord God of Israel liveth, before whom I stand, there shall not be dew nor rain these years, but according to my word."

We reach the heart of the matter when we turn to the Gospels. Most significant is the name that John gives Jesus: "The Word." The Word which created all things. "The Word made flesh." Nowhere does the authority of the spoken word of faith come out so clearly as in His life, which was a constant series of such spoken words with their miraculous results. To the waves: "Peace, be still." To a fever: a rebuke. To the fig tree: a curse. To the evil spirit: "I charge thee, come out of him." To the nobleman: "Go thy way, thy son liveth." To the cripple: "Rise, take up thy bed and walk." To the centurion: "As thou hast believed, so be it done unto thee." To the leper: "Be thou clean." At the grave of Lazarus, to His Father: "I thank Thee that Thou hast heard me"; then, to Lazarus: "Come forth." No wonder they were amazed at the authority with which He spoke. No wonder we echo the officer's words: "Never man spake like this Man."

The centurion seemed to be the one person who sensed the power that resided in that word, when he so boldly broke through the customary idea that the physical presence of the Saviour was necessary, and suggested that He need not come in person to his house, but just speak the word and his servant would be healed. It was a penetration into the secrets of faith which just thrilled the

Saviour, and brought those words of highest commendation to His lips: "Verily I say unto you, I have not found so great faith, no, not in Israel"; and gave him a momentary glimpse of the universality of the coming Church: "And I say unto you that many shall come from the east and west, and shall sit down with Abraham and Isaac and Jacob, in the kingdom of heaven."

The Lord Jesus Himself revealed the secret in that vitally important record of His conversation with His disciples after the fig-tree incident.[1] This is the one outstanding occasion on which He pointed out that He Himself was using the word of faith, and that they ought to do the same. When Peter commented on the withered fig tree to which He had said the day before: "No man eat fruit of thee hereafter for ever", He told them to "have faith in God" and they could do the same. In other words, that the way He performed His miracles was by this word of faith, which they could use just as much as He; but He then went on to make clear that it was a *spoken word* of faith, and not just an aspiration, request or hope; for they were to *say* to a mountain: "Be thou removed", and not to doubt in their hearts, and thy would have whatsoever they said. He explained at the same time that such a spoken word of faith was the central act that mattered in the prayer life, for He divided the process of prayer into four component parts—desire, request, faith that the thing is done, and realization; but all is made parenthetic to the central emphasis, the summit of the mountain: "Believe that ye receive" then and there. On one other occasion He stressed the same truth when He said that with faith as a grain of mustard seed they could "say" the word of command to a sycamine tree and it would obey.

That the apostles followed this out is obvious from the

[1] Mark 11: 12-24.

early days when the Master gave them authority over evil spirits and to heal sicknesses, telling them later that what they bound on earth would be bound in heaven, and what they loosed would be loosed.

The actual expression "the word of faith" is used by Paul (Romans 10: 8) when expounding the faith that justifies; and here he brings out exactly the same truth: that faith is something which must have plain-spoken expression. Hope or desire is not enough. The prayer of request is not enough. Not even the belief in the heart. What is believed in the inner man must issue from the mouth. "If thou shalt confess with thy mouth the Lord Jesus" is the summit reached. And this truth is traced by Paul right back to a revelation in the earliest days of recorded history—to Moses' comment in the book of Deuteronomy.

If it is asked why there must be such emphasis on the spoken word of faith, the answer may be partly beyond our reach. It is hidden in the mysteries of creation. All we are told is that the Son is the Word, and that by the Word are all things made—The Word, presumably, of the Father.[1] Therefore we know that the spoken word (not the deed) is the creating power; the word is antecedent to the deed, and therefore more powerful and more important. Indeed, the word produces the deed. Thus the first act of God of which there is record is a spoken word which began the creating process: "Let there be light", and there was light. And this was followed by six other "words", each of which produced a corresponding new state in creation.

Now a word is a crystallization of a thought; we can see as far as that. Thought is fluid, unformed. We turn things over in our mind. The word gives definition to the

[1] "God in thought, the Father; God in Word, the Son; God in Act, the Spirit." From *The Lord as Truth*, by Alan Fairweather.

thought. The spoken word, given in the form of a command or decision, expresses the idea in the mind, digested, clarified, authoritative. A man's word, we say, is his bond. A general's word is his command, after he has weighed all the various possible disposals of his forces. An architect's word is his plan. An engineer's word is his blueprint. It is final, creative. It sets action in motion. James tells us of the power for good or evil of the spoken word which sets the course of nature on fire.

Exactly what the spoken word of faith effects we do not know. The nearest we can say is that it is the spiritual act of taking and using. Faith is the spiritual hand. Exactly as, in the natural world, nothing is received and put to use merely by wishing or hoping or asking for it, but by taking and using it, so in the spiritual. The hand must reach out and take the food or the book. Faith must reach out and take the promises, and the public evidence of such taking is the spoken word of faith. Probably the effect in the realm of the Spirit is exactly the same as in the realm of matter. God offers all in His promises. The word of faith is the act of taking and applying His power according to need. What we actually take we actually have, and when the decisive word of faith has been spoken, God in His grace begins to work; and as the stand of faith is persisted in, the answer appears.

That is just why the declared word of faith is so vital and should be so stressed.[1] It is the act of taking in the

---

1 All that is here said of the word of faith needs, of course, the counter-balancing emphasis which the letter of James gives to those of Paul: "What doth it profit though a man say he hath faith, and have not works? . . . Yea, a man may say, Thou hast faith, and I have works: show me thy faith without thy works, and I will show thee my faith by my works . . . but wilt thou know, O vain man, that faith without works is dead?"

The word of faith, if a mere word, can be a hollow sham. Faith is invisible, and we suggest that the serious lack in so much of our prayer life, both public and private, is that it hardly gets beyond the stage of asking. Hardly ever do we hear a person in a public prayer meeting, having asked, take and thank; yet probably it is much more important to have "taking" meetings than "asking" meetings. Our constant asking must have the same effect on God as would a child on his parents, who keeps asking for food, when they have set his meal before him and told him to take and eat it.

the whole man in action, and the word of faith includes the heart and mind that is in tune with the will of God and His written revelation, the voice that speaks the word of faith, and all subsequent action that is in full conformity with the position of faith which has been declared.

Empty words of faith can be spoken, which have no living faith and thus no saving power in them, such as the Roman Catholic priest who claims that he performs the miracle of transubstantiation by the word of consecration, and that he looses the sinner from his sin by the word of absolution.

Chapter Eighteen

(i) In Major Matters

SUCH a bold use of the word of faith however must obviously raise one query in our minds which needs most careful examination. How and when can I, a mere mortal, dare to declare with certainty that God will do this or that? Must I not always add: "If it is His will?" And does not that immediately make such a declaration of faith impossible, for the whole essence of it is its certainty?

It is evident, from all the Scriptural examples already quoted, that these men knew some way of settling their doubts, for there is no sign whatever, in their declarations, of questioning whether God would do it or not, whether it was His will or not. Clearly they had resolved that problem. How?

We have reached the major problem in the use of prayer and faith in the daily life. How many people would be only too glad to be sure that their prayers are being answered and to be able to say so. What loads would be off people's hearts and minds. How infectious would be their joy and confidence. How keen their anticipations. Yet is exactly what John says is to be our normal experience: that we are to have confidence because: "if we ask anything according to His will, He heareth us; and if we know that He hear us, we know that we have the petitions that we desired of Him",[1] no matter what we have asked. Obviously, John implied that it should be a normal

[1] John 5: 14, 15.

thing with us to ask according to His will, on which all the rest depends, and therefore that we should know how to discern what is His will before we ask.

What then is the solution to the problem? There are two main categories in which God's will has to be sought and found; or rather, in very many cases, in which God has to get His will through to us when we are not looking an inch beyond our own noses. The first concerns the great moments of our lives, the major crises and choices.

It is obvious that in such matters we must know without a doubt, and there must be a way by which we can and do know. God, indeed, does have means of making a way so plain to us that neither man nor devil nor our own trembling hearts can shake our certainty. The ways in which the Lord "appeared" to many in the Bible and "spoke" to many are examples of this: Abraham bidden to leave his country; Moses at the burning bush; Gideon commanded to defeat Midian; David inquiring of the Lord and receiving answers; the prophet that gave God's word to Jehoshaphat after a day of national prayer and fasting, that he need not fight in the battle against the invading foe; Paul and Barnabas set apart by the Holy Ghost for the ministry; Paul summoned to Macedonia in a dream.

To find God's mind on such occasions, when there is time to seek it and when a clear understanding of it is a necessity, all depends on the determination not to act until one is certain. Patience is the key. And patience is not an elementary grace in the Christian life, but a sign of maturity. "Let patience have her perfect work that ye may be perfect and entire, wanting nothing", says James. For patience means being emptied of all self-activity, having victory over the urge to make a snap decision, and refusing to be rushed into taking this or that to be God's way without the crystal clear assurance within that it really is so.

The issue is clear. Does God "speak" to-day to His sons as He did of old to His servants? The Old Testament particularly is dotted all over with instances of men declaring that "the Lord said" this or that to them, and there are equally clear incidents in the Acts. We may take it that, in the centuries before the Holy Ghost was poured forth at Pentecost and all believers henceforth knew the indwelling and inner witness, before it was revealed that God's people *have* the mind of Christ and an unction from the Holy One, by which they "know all things and need not that any man teach them", and before the written Scriptures were in our hands, God had to use more startling ways to convey His word to His servants. He would use vision, dream, visual appearance, or some clear form of voice; or maybe the inner hearing of those outstanding souls who are the marked men of the Old Testament was unusually good, both because of their intimate walk with God in great surrounding darkness, and because their lack of other helps we have in Gospel days made their inner ear especially sensitive, just as the blind develop special ways of "seeing".

We cannot go with those who say that those days were peculiar, and that even the ways by which God spoke to His servants after Pentecost He has long since ceased to use, and that therefore to-day we must not expect God to convey His will to us in any more direct or personal form than by the general principles of His Word. Thousands and tens of thousands give the lie to this, who have humbly endeavoured to live their lives by His direct leading.

But it is true to say that His ways of communicating His truth to man to-day are much more regularized and discernible. It is no longer, from man's point of view, a matter of sudden and uncertain revelation, such as the poet pictured:

> *Yet ever and anon a trumpet sounds*
> *From the hid battlements of Eternity;*
> *Those shaken mists a space unsettle, then*
> *Round the half-glimpsed turrets slowly wash again.*

What were unpredictable visitations from on high are now, by God's grace, the mind of Christ indwelling His people. God's voice in His people and in His Word is permanently present and always speaking. It is not a matter of waiting for a voice from Heaven, but of waiting for ourselves to be quiet enough to hear the ever-speaking voice within and glimpse the clearly-manifested way.

God does speak as He spoke of old, but by somewhat different methods. Then He had to break through to man's mind as best He could. Now, through Christ, He indwells a man's mind and can turn it, when yielded and open, and, above all, when it recognizes the truth about His abiding presence, quietly, continually, certainly in the way of His planning. "It seemed good to the Holy Ghost and to us", wrote the Church in Jerusalem, and that is as good a description as can be of the co-operative guidance of the new creation, through the inter-action of God's mind and ours.

When, therefore, a major problem arises, the way of obtaining the guidance already there in the invisible is first to keep the track clear from the bias of our own thinking, our own willing. We are human. We are bound to have our own thoughts and desires, and for that very reason it often takes time to be free of them. Thought and desire are right and necessary if integrated with His thinking and His willing. To get the "I" and the "my" out of them, which may be opposed to Him, is the trouble.

That was Christ's battle at Gethsemane, and the greatest of all illustrations of what we mean. God's will was always there. The will which sent His beloved Son into the world. But in the blackness of that valley of the shadow which He was entering, with His soul exceeding sorrowful unto death, He cried out: "O my Father, if it be possible, let this cup pass from me: nevertheless not as I will, but as Thou wilt." It was the voice of human agony, which would not be human if it did not shrink from its ordeal, and for a time it clouded the clear apprehension of the Divine will by the human spirit. Three hours of intensest travail so immersed the human in the divine that He was able to say: "The cup which My Father hath given me, shall I not drink it?" The mind of the Father had never varied. The mind of the Son, oppressed by the greatest load that ever human heart was called to carry, had to fight its way through to a clear sight of and acquiescence in the appointed way.

To find God's mind does not mean an emptied human mind or a desireless human heart, but that the mind and heart are exercised, not to cling to their own ways, but to yield them up, to die to them; then to substitute for them a search for God's way. Ponder over what indications there are of the way God is leading. Think and pray them over. Use the mind; it is given to reason, analyse, select. And the heart; it is given to have living desire, to quicken the will into action; but let it be set on delighting itself in the Lord and running the way of His commandments.

But, above all, let there be no confusion between our thinking and desiring, and His inspoken word. The difference between them is the difference between light and darkness. One issues from the human soul; the other breaks forth in the spirit. Only the spiritual, the Spirit-born, can tell the difference, but they can tell it—infallibly. Paul said that, when he told the Corinthians that the "natural man receiveth not the things of the Spirit of God, neither can he know them, because they are spiritually discerned. But he that is spiritual discerneth all things." Moses knew the difference when he told the Israelites on one occasion that they would see that day that the Lord had sent him to do all these works, "for I have not done them of my own mind".[1]

It is here that the patience we spoke of above is needed. God is light and His word in our spirit is light: "like a clear heat after rain, like a cloud of dew in the heat of harvest." The least obscurity, the least vestige of doubt, the faintest element of drive or pressure in the spirit, is clear evidence that God's word has not yet shone fully into our hearts. The peace of God, says Paul, is to "sit as an umpire"[2] in our hearts; the peace, in other words, will be the clear verdict that "this is the way, walk ye in it". Till then, wait, and however hardly pressed, tell the Lord that we are His servants and that the servant is duty bound to obey, but first has the right to plain orders. Till he gets these, he cannot, and cannot be expected to, act.

The use of the Scriptures in getting God's mind may be twofold. God may give us the light we seek by a verse in the course of our reading. We would expect this to be so, if we are those who continually soak our minds in His Word. There are instances by the thousand of this. It has, of course, its dangers, as the mind that is desiring a certain end can very easily see Scriptures that suit its outlook and claim them as a divine seal. The safeguard is to see that not only are there Scriptures which give encouragement along that certain line, but also that circumstances and

[1] Num. 16: 28.   [2] Col. 3: 15 (Literal Translation).

the weighing up of evidence seem all to point in the same direction. Mature fellow-Christians can also be consulted, not as if their word is final, but as additional confirmation if in agreement, or as warning against precipitancy if in disapproval.

But stil the final word is in the heart of the seeker. He has the mind of Christ and the unction from the Holy One, and the golden rule is to refuse to move, even if a dozen confirmations are asked for, until not a vestige of doubt remains. Humbly, yet boldly, we are to wait until we can say, as much as God's servants of old: "Thus saith the Lord to me."

Chapter Nineteen

(ii) In Minor Matters

WE have now examined the way "the Word of the Lord" comes to us in matters of decisive importance. But, for many, it is in the more ordinary affairs of everyday life that they find such difficulty in knowing the will of God, and in having any conception about the things that they could confidently take by faith. There is a household need of food, or home, or money, or furniture, or job. There are the unsaved children. There are health questions. There are the hundred and one problems connected with our sphere of business, Christian service, our neighbours, our relatives. Life would be too short anyhow for us to obtain a clear word from God as to what would be His will in each matter, and often the call for action is too sudden. How then can we possibly pray in faith, still less use the word of authority, when we do not know God's will, and the Scriptures make it so plain that confident prayer depends upon asking according to His will?

The men of the Bible again give us the clue. In two whose activities are given us in some detail we see the point most clearly; also in the life of the Lord Jesus. We can watch both Moses and Elisha when various sudden demands are made on them, demands that come in the natural course of their lives. Moses, as leader of Israel, is suddenly called upon for bread and water; he is brought up without warning against the barrier of the Red Sea and the unexpected pursuit of the Egyptian Army. He has to meet a surprise attack by the Amalekites. And so on. In Elisha's life the point comes out in still more homely fashion. A widow of one of his assistants is in financial difficulties. A pot of stew is poisoned by mistake. One of his students loses his borrowed axe-head. Exactly the same type of sudden demand is laid on Christ; the disciples sinking in a storm, the multitude with no food: the leper, the blind, the suppliant father and mother, falling at His feet.

In few of these cases is there any indication that a period of retirement was sought in order to find the mind of God, although there were certainly critical moments when it is said of Moses, for instance, that he fell on his face; probably because on these occasions he was faced with outbreaks or revolt or loud complaint, and needed to quieten his spirit before he could speak the word of the Lord unmixed with his own personal reactions. The same is noticeable in Elisha when sent for by the idolatrous King Jehoram, with whom the godly King Jehoshaphat had allied himself. "What have I to do with thee?" said he indignantly to Jehoram. "Get thee to the prophets of thy father." And when only persuaded to stay for Jehoshaphat's sake, he asked for a minstrel to soothe his rightly ruffled spirit, before he could know and give out the Lord's word.

But the striking fact is that normally these men of God, as in the case of the Saviour Himself, took the supply of God for a sudden emergency in their stride, as it were. They took it for granted that where need was, there also was divine supply, if they would simply draw on it. Look at Elisha providing the oil, healing the fountain, raising the axe-head, getting the water for the army, and so on. But what was special revelation to them is meant to be common grace to us, "the mystery which hath been hid from ages and from generations but now is made manifest to His saints... which is Christ in you." To us it is now said that "it is God that worketh in you both to will and to do of His good pleasure." Here lies the secret. The life in Christ is not to be regarded as a life lived by jerks, sometimes in and sometimes out of His will. That is exactly the esoteric view of God which remains with us as graveclothes from the fall—that God is merely outside us, transcendent, and His will must be interpreted to us by a constant process of revelations, infusions, breakings forth of light into the midst of a normal experience of darkness. God is transcendent, but, such is the glorious paradox of faith, He is also immanent. Gradually we must come familair with the esoteric truth, Christ *in* you, joined to the Lord one spirit, God dwelling in us and walking in us:[1] "The anointing which ye have received of Him abideth in you"; "It is God that worketh in you to will"; and God's guidance must be seen more in the daily direction of our wills and desires than in sudden words and inspirations.

We must dare to believe that our wills and desires are His, God working them in us, unless we are definitely conscious that they are opposed to Him. Usually we take the other attitude, that our wills and desires are not His, but just our own, and probably selfish, except in the rare cases when we have His will directly communicated to us. It is there that our bondage and hesitation comes over the interpretation of His will. Jesus spoke quietly and naturally to His disciples about asking anything from Him in His Name, stressing that whatever they asked He would give them, and gently chiding them that up till then they had asked nothing. John, who quoted these sayings of Jesus in his Gospel, repeated the same in his own letters

[1] 2 Cor. 6: 16.

"Whatsoever we ask we receive of Him"; "If we ask anything according to His will he heareth us." Christ (and John) said this just because He was taking it for granted that their *normal desires* would be His will, and thus asked in His Name. In that same talk He spoke to them of vine and branches, explained that that was now their natural relationship to Him, and that all they needed to do was to take care to maintain it. If they did that, then the sap of His mind, His will and desires, would naturally flow through their hearts, and they would without effort be willing one will and desiring one desire with Him.

John perceived the oversensitiveness of the redeemed human heart and its tendency to false self-condemnation, which would prevent it from acting easily and naturally in the Spirit, and would always make it afraid of itself, fearful of presumption, over-suspicious of selfish motives, causing a paralysis of bold faith and prayer; so he added a passage in his letter on this specific point in connection with believing prayer.[1] He here said that our normal condition should be one of confidence before God, confidence in prayer that what we ask for we get. But unfortunately, he said, we get so easily under self-condemnation and are tortured by it. "Our hearts condemn us", and then we hardly dare believe that Christ still indwells us, much less that He grants our desires; so John adds that God is greater than our hearts, and knows the real truth and acts according to that truth, and not according to our wrongful self-condemnation. But, all the same, a self-condemning heart, he says, does make it impossible for us to enjoy His presence, to be bold and free and happy in our acts and attitudes, or to declare the word of faith. And so in a later chapter,[2] he again refers to this false and tormenting fear and self-accusation, and gives the remedy for it.

[1] 1 John 3: 19-22.   [2] 1 John 4: 17, 18.

Do you love God? Does God love you? Well then, stand in that love. Realize that such love has no fear in it. Refuse the fear that torments. Revel in the perfect love' then dare to count on it and act on it.

One of the devil's favourite weapons with immature Christians is false accusation, producing self-torment. Before we are saved, he would keep God's voice away from us altogether, if he could. If he cannot and if we respond to the divine voice in conviction and conversion, then he uses another method. He transforms himself into an angel of light, pretends to speak to us with God's voice, knowing that we will quickly and sensitively respond. He constantly enlarges on our faults and failings, points out every vestige of self in us, keeps us mourning over ourselves till we wonder whether God can have any more to do with us. Thousands of God's people are kept out of the wealth of their heritage by this means. Instead of the spirit of adoption which makes us feel so at home with God that we call Him "Abba Father", the equivalent of the modern "Daddy", we are kept in the spirit of bondage again to fear. We live by the crumbs of God's grace picked up beneath the table, rather than as those who sit at meat with Him, the glorified Jesus supping with us and we with Him.

The way to distinguish between these two voices, that of God and Satan, is indicated by John in this passage. The voice of the enemy, bringing fear and condemnation, always torments. There is no fear, no torment, in love. Therefore when our inmost thoughts produce bondage and distress, pain and depression, we can always know they are from the pit. It is the voice of the stranger which the sheep are not to know. When God is speaking, there is light and peace, assurance and largeness in our hearts, even though the Voice may have in it a word of rebuke.

God's rebukes are redemptive, pointing upwards to cleansing and renewal. Satan's rebukes are destructive, pointing downwards to damnation and despair.

What, then, we learn from Moses and Elisha, and from Jesus the Son of Man, is that, unless we are consciously opposed to God in heart, the supply of our daily needs *is* His will; such indeed is the meaning of the prayer for our daily bread. Just where we are is God's plan for us, and just what we need where we are is what God would give us. Our environment is our opportunity. Our environment provides both the material and justification for boldness of faith. All that Moses or Elisha, or the Lord Himself, did was to meet the sudden next need of daily life with a taking-for-granted faith that the Father would supply, and a declaration of that faith, and such action as was the natural consequence of such faith. Let us learn to do the same. Is it an unsaved soul in our midst? Is it a financial problem, a new job needed, a supply of food or clothing? Is it a harvest of souls in our ministry or Bible Class? Let us be bold to make the declaration of faith. It is far more honouring to God to believe than to doubt Him, and a far bigger blessing to our neighbour. The men of old would even corner God. "You cannot fail us", Moses would say. "If You do, the world will say You could not deliver us. So You have got to work for us!" God loves language like that! "Nail Him down", as one preacher used to say. It is only a heart full of perfect love and faith that can talk like that; but God would far rather have rough and homely language out of a full heart, than the politest and most respectful phrases which do not come much deeper than from the lips or brain.

Jesus Himself made a staggering statement to this effect. He said that a praying person should be like someone who is so determined to get what he wants that he sets his teeth and makes a proper nuisance of himself till he gets it: wakes up his neighbour at midnight; disregards the warning that his knocking will wake the children; knocks even louder when he hears this, because he knows that it will bring his unwilling neighbour downstairs in double-quick time to stop the racket; and finally gets, not just three loaves, but all he wanted to take, from doubtless a very exasperated donor. Not, indeed, Jesus comments, because he was his friend, but because of his sheer "cheek" (the word used literally means "shamelessness"). And if an unwilling friend can thus be forced to be generous, what about a willing Father? Surely Christ exhorts, not to caution and hesitation, but to great boldness in prayer, yet coupled with great humility.

Chapter Twenty

FALSE FAITH

LIKE anything else, such truths concerning finding God's will can be abused. But so could Paul's emphasis on justification by faith. He did not, however, for that reason refrain from stating the truth. He knew that if there were a few who would turn the grace of God into lascivousness, misinterpreting liberty as licence, there were multitudes of others who would revel in and rightly use the glorious liberty of the children of God.

So it is in the truth of the endless resources of God at the disposal of faith, and the fact that faith can be exercised to supply the every-day desires of every-day life. Some few will seek the quails and get them with leanness to their souls, for there is a Satanic as well as a God-centred, Spirit-guided faith, a faith that can remove mountains but which is not motivated by divine love. There is a sense in which faith is a law of nature, which can be operated on another level under the control of another spirit, motivated by self-will and self-love with purely selfish ends. There is a god of this world as well as the God and Father of our Lord Jesus Christ. There is an evil spirit which now worketh in the children of disobedience, as well as the Holy Spirit. There is a prince of this world who has resources at his disposal, the kingdom, power and glory which he offered Jesus, and which he said that he would give to whom he would.

All forms of human achievement are by faith, as has

already been pointed out. All draw on the resources of the universe, material, mental, spiritual. The building of a business, the carrying through to success of an enterprise, great or small, the acquirement of knowledge, all require faith in varying degrees and on differing levels. There are regular "spiritual" sciences[1] which are built on this truth. They have their followers and their large measure of success; indeed, they have lessons that they could teach us in the practice of faith. But their foundations are devillish, not divine, for few of them will confess that "Jesus Christ is come in the flesh" and that "Jesus is the Son of God", the tests given by John by which we are to "try the spirits whether they are God".

Sorcery, witchcraft, black magic, and such-like practices, work on the same principle, only that they acknowledge the direct intercourse of faith with "wicked spirits in heavenly places", and openly draw their power from them; whereas the teachers of "spiritual science" are much more subtle, in that they centre their doctrine on one aspect of God which they take to the utmost extreme, to the exclusion of the counter-balancing aspect which is equally stressed in the Scriptures.

They are an example of the pitfalls which yawn before those who do not open their minds to every aspect of the truth revealed in God's Word. They select with delight that phase of truth which specially appeals to them, and run upon it as hidden treasure. They explore and develop it until they seem to see it alone on every page of Scripture, to the exclusion of anything which seems to give an opposite point of view; and what could have been a healthy re-emphasis to the Church of Christ of some truth which has been neglected is transmuted instead into deadly error.

[1] Christian Science, New Thought, Unity, and others.

Thus these teachers, who have something real to say to us on the immanence of God, *could* be a healthy counter-balance to an overemphasis on His transcendence (which leaves so many Christians with a sense of distance from Him, and consequent weakness, diffidence, joylessness). They rightly see God as the One Mind behind all creation, the I AM who is in and through everything, the Life of all lives; but, in thus concentrating upon His immanence, they neglect the equally necessary truth of His transcendence, His separate being, His dwelling in the light which no man can approach unto. They carry to the furthest extreme the teachings of the mystics on the unity of the soul with God: to a point beyond that which in most cases the mystics themselves would have intended it to be taken; for it must be remembered that those giant spirits, to whom we give the name of mystics,[1] are men and women through the centuries who have left us at the foothills, while they have climbed the spiritual uplands and stood in the presence of God. They have been caught up with Paul into the third heaven and heard things hardly lawful to be uttered, and struggled to put into words what language can hardly contain. Their written testimonies, glowing with heavenly fervour, are one of the richest legacies of the Church of God on earth; but in the rapture of their experiennce, almost blinded by the light of their heavenly visions, it may well be that their hearts have sometimes gone further than their heads, and their theology needs counterbalancing by the more objective sides of truth.

[1] For example: John of the Cross, John of Ruysbroeck, St. Teresa, Francis of Assisi, Jacob Boehme, William Law, Pascal, Mme. Guyon, Meister Eckhart, John Tauler, Henry Suso, Catherine of Sienna, Angela de Foligno, Richard Rolle, Lady Julian of Norwich, and the unknown authors of *Theologica Germanica* and *The Cloud of Unknowing.*

Teachings such as these, twisted often out of their full context, and such as would be themselves repudiated by these humble but great souls, coupled with forms of philosophy such as Hegel's idealistic monism, and even with concepts that are really derived from Buddhism and Hinduism, form the basis of a theology, at bottom anthropocentric rather than theocentric, which gives no place to the plain dualism of the Bible, and as a consequence approaches to the edge of pantheism. God practically loses His separate entity as a Person. He is One with the universe which is His "body". Man is the self-realization of God. Man in essence is God incarnate. Man at the centre of his being is eternally one with God, is God.

Then, to bolster up this extreme position, and to account for the plain and horrible contradictions to such statements in man as we see him through history, the explanation is given that man is in ignorance of his true self. Foolishly regarding himself as a separate being who must fight his own lone battle in an unfriendly world, and surrounded by other people as separate and alone as himself, and each out to get the best for himself, he uses all his resources to gain his own ends. Here, they say, is the origin of evil. It is ignorance, not wickedness. It is just a misuse of good, not an enmity against a personal God. It is merely negation, nothing; not the power of darkness derived from a kingdom and king of darkness; and in saying this they join hands with the rationalists and humanists and modernists of all the centuries.[1]

---

[1] This fundamentally erroneous view of man, which maintains his essential goodness, and attributes his "failures" either to ignorance, or to his body warring against his mind, or to environment, has been Satan's most devastating and far-reaching method of pouring scorn on man's need of a Saviour. It has been the point of view that "the world"

There is value, they say, in Jesus as the one perfect "Initiate". He alone walked this earth spotlessly, in full-ness of light as to His (and man's) essential oneness with the Father. He, they say, rightly called Himself the Son of God, to reveal to us that we are all sons. He knew the secret of the divine resources available to all the sons of God by virtue of their Christhood. He exercised and ap-plied this secret of faith, and spoke out into manifestation those hidden powers of healing and supply. Some would even go so far as to teach that His Cross is the most vital "lesson" ever taught to mankind, for by it He revealed that by death and resurrection is the way to realized Sonship. Each man who in ignorance lives as a lone self and acts on the principle of self-seeking as the correct way of life, must "die" to himself and "rise" to the spirit of love and life within him; recognize his unity with the Spirit of all

---

has always held, and still does, and always will. It can be traced in varying forms from Greek thought as represented by Plato and Aris-totle, through the Roman era as represented by the Stoics, on to the Renaissance and Enlightenment where, through Rousseau and such writers, it became the foundation stone of modern humanism. Only the Bible has withstood it and pointed, not to man's ignorance, but to his deliberate rebellion against God as the source of his troubles. The Reformation, as opposed to the Renaissance, re-emphasized this funda-mental Bible truth.

Modernism and Liberalism has this same worm at its roots. It has attempted to synthesize this rationalistic lie of man's basic goodness with certain aspects of New Testament truth, and as a consequence produced its sinless, bloodless, Saviourless "Gospel" of Jesus as man's example, and of a world which would gradually be leavened by Christianity until the Millennial Age is finally reached.

The convulsions and horrors of the past thirty years have done much to shake and shatter these erroneous concepts, combined with the theo-logical teachings and writings of such men as Kierkegaard, Karl Barth, and Emil Brunner. Perhaps the best modern writer on the whole subject is Reinhold Niebuhr. See his *Nature and Destiny of Man.*

life, use his prerogative of creative faith to draw to himself his visible needs from invisible resources, to dissolve hatred and evil around him by his own output of positive love and good. No greater word, they say, has been spoken than that word of Jesus: "Whosoever shall save his life shall lose it; and whosoever shall lose his life shall find it."

But all this, although it has some very helpful lessons to teach us of the reality of our oneness with God (only through Christ) and the privilege and powers of this relationship, has so completely ignored the other side of truth that the whole teaching has become a seductive error; its source, as a consequence, is found to be in the subtilty and wisdom of the serpent instead of in the grace and power of God. For the existence of God as a separate living Person, "The high and holy One who inhabiteth eternity", practically disappears. The disobedience of man, the existence of the devil, sin as a reality, man's responsibility before God, God's wrath and judgment, the reality of hell as well as heaven; God's love revealed in sending His only begotten Son into the world, Christ's essential sonship and deity, His blood atonement and physical ressurrection, His all-sufficient Saviourhood; man's repentance, justification, sonship, and sanctification in Christ; and, finally, Christ's second coming; all these cease to be truths through the neglect and denial of the one great basic truth of the transcendence of God as well as His immanence, of a dualism as well as a monism; for the final truth to finite man is paradox, it is unreconciled contraries existing side by side, and each essential to a faith which would keep to the high road of truth; illogicalities to the mind, which the Spirit transcends, the dialectic of infinity which he that is spiritual can discern though he cannot explain. In such ways as these can guidance and faith and like precious truths be misused, and can become the metaphysical armoury of religious systems whose author is "Satan himself transformed into an angel of light."

Chapter Twenty-One

STRATEGY IN FAITH

BUT to return to our subject, on speaking the word of faith. If we are to do so, if we are to be bold in believing that in many circumstances of our daily life what we want is what He wants us to have,[1] for He is working in us to will and to do of His good pleasure, then there remains one important prerequisite.

Nothing is easier in the rough and tumble of life than to remain on the natural level and never even to conceive of bringing spiritual forces to bear on a situation. Obviously no word of faith can be spoken, no investigation even made into the will or plan of God as a groundwork for speaking it, unless it first dawns on the mind that there is some better condition than the existing one, that God can intervene and change things. That seems to go without saying. Yet it is a blank wall which hinders God from intervening as He would in a million instances.

Look only at the Scriptures. Why only an Abraham whom God could call out to start a new generation of faith? Why only a Moses who could get bread and water in a wilderness? Why only a David who could defeat Goliath? Or only a Gideon to destroy the Midianites? Or only an Elijah to turn the nation back to God? Was it because God has favourites, and will do for one what He will not for another? The answer to that is obvious. God's whosoevers and whensoevers have no limits. The truth

[1] There are some real problems in this respect, such as sickness and death, which we consider in a later chapter (Chap. 22).

is that very rarely can God find an individual emancipated enough from his normal outlook to glimpse even the possibility of change. "The eyes of the Lord run to and fro throughout the whole earth," the prophet said, "to shew Himself strong in the behalf of them whose heart is perfect toward Him." The others in David's or Gideon's or Elijah's day just didn't see that God could and would do the impossible if someone would rise up and believe him. Blindness is the problem. Preoccupation with and resignation to the *status quo*. We are all guilty of it a thousand times.

To see things from the human aspect, to feel the weight of things, the apparent impossibility of any change, is not wrong. It is just natural. We should be sub-human if we did not. Indeed, as we pointed out in the chapter on temptation, the pressure of things upon us is the first step in an essential process:

> *Why comes temptation, but for man to meet*
> *And master and make crouch beneath his feet*
> *And to be pedestall'd in triumph?*

It is the friction which kindles the flame of faith. Paul points this out when he says that in the ministry of the Gospel, trouble, perplexity, persecution, calamity, come to us as an essential stage in the production of the spiritual harvest.[1] The old life dies *that* the new may spring forth, we "bearing about in the body the dying of the Lord Jesus *that* the life also of Jesus might be made manifest in our body". That resurrection life, Paul says, first wells up in the soul (the seed) itself in an unconquerable spirit of faith, which gives almost an india-rubber consistency to the soul. There is trouble, yes, but never panic;

[1] 2 Cor. 4: 8-12.

perplexity, yes, but never hopelessness; persecution, but never a sense of abandonment; knock-down, but never knock-out blows. And then it becomes the world's spiritual granary. "Death worketh in us, but life in *you*." The seed dies. The harvest rises. The world is fed.

But the trouble is that so often we just do not "see" this. Life is a constant series of glorious opportunities not grasped because not recognized. We just take the happenings of life for granted and leave them there. We are so used to judging by our natural senses, to seeing need, weakness, frustration, with the helpless, unbelieving outlook of the world. We find it unnatural and difficult to carry out Christ's word "Judge not by appearances".

There is only one remedy. In warfare no army can fight without a general staff. No battle is won right up at the front line. It is too close to the enemy to get a right perspective. Soldiers may make fun of "the brass hats", as they nickname the staff, but they could not do without them. Back there at general headquarters, away from the roar of battle, the commander-in-chief has his maps and reports, holds his conferences and issues his orders. Tactics, the clash of regiment with regiment, tank with tank, are useless without strategy, the over-all plan of campaign.

Life's battle must also have its strategy. Blind tactics, desultory front-line shooting, is mere waste of ammunition. There must be that quiet spot, that G.H.Q. away in a wood, where the war is reviewed as a whole and the voice of the C.-in-C. is heard. Not just a blind "Stick-it, boys" or "Fire-away"; but "How can we relieve the pressure? When can we counter-attack? What about a shift of the army? A sudden drive on this flank or that?"

See Jehoshaphat, king of Judah, when he was suddenly attacked by a confederacy of enemies, Ammonites, Edomites, Moabites. They were on him without warning. The first he knew was that they were only thirty miles from the capital. Common sense would say: "Mobilize, rush out and stop them"; yet with little hope, for they vastly outnumbered him and were prepared for battle. But Jehoshaphat knew the secret of the spiritual strategist. Don't rush *out*. Rush *in*. Go to the C.-in-C. Have it out with Him. Get His outlook and orders.

Jehoshaphat was human. He feared, the record says. Quite right, quite normal. Necessary, in fact, for fear is faith in reverse; and faith, once roused to believe the worst, can be reversed to believe the opposite. Paul feared when he came to Corinth after his rough handling in Philippi and Thessalonica; but he converted his fear into a boomerang and made it the driving force of a greater determination than ever before to preach none other "save Jesus Christ, and Him crucified".[1] Even Jesus feared, but the fear aroused "strong crying and tears", and the crying an overcoming faith. He "was heard in that He feared".[2]

Jehoshaphat also used his fear aright. He did not allow it to give him spiritual paralysis by flooding his mind with counsels of panic and exhausting his energies on futile preparations. He did not allow it to hold him a captive in the power of appearances. He took the way by which the panic-stricken soul struggles up from the grim dungeon of satanic threats to the bracing highlands of God's deliverances, from the cry of terror to the laugh of faith, from shoulders bowed beneath the load of care to bruising the enemy beneath the feet. He called the nation to a day of fasting and prayer. Not to front-line action, but to staff consultations. It was the strategist at work; the day of tactics had not yet come. It was the general calling his staff together to meet the threat of invasion.

[1] 1 Cor. 2: 2, 3.   [2] Heb. 5: 7.

But now note the contents of his prayer which the record quotes in full.[1] He did not reach his specific request until the last sentence. All the rest was asking obvious questions of God, the affirmative answer to each of which was equally obvious. "Art not Thou God in heaven?" "Rulest not Thou over all?" "In Thine hand is there not power and might so that none is able to withstand Thee?" Then, a little closer home: "Art not Thou *our* God Who didst drive out the inhabitants of this land before thy people Israel, and gavest it to the seed of Abraham Thy friend for ever?" "And didst Thou not say that if, when evil cometh, we cry unto Thee, Thou wilt hear and help?"

What was Jehoshaphat really doing? Not persuading God, but himself! Piling up in his own mind in God's presence an overwhelming weight of evidence that God had given him a right to appeal to Him in this case. Finding, in fact, a foothold for faith. And that brings us to the real roots of effectual prayer. It comes from God first to me, and then back from me to God. It is God who has purpose to fulfil, in the destruction of the devil's work, in shewing forth His glory and grace to men; it is God who permits this or that experience to come to us: and then, if we will listen, it is God who tells us how He will glorify His Name and confound the devil by getting us out of it. We may appear to be crying to Him to deliver; but what really is happening is that, as we reason and plead and present His promises to Him, the Spirit is getting through to us and conveying to us the sure fact that God has long ago planned the answer. He knows what we have need of before we ask. He responds before we call. In other words, while we are busy persuading God, in reality He is persuading us! For what He wants is our

[1] 2 Chron. 20: 1-30.

faith; but faith is not easily attained in times of stress and bewilderment, for faith is hearing God's voice and believing Him, and the troubled mind may need to pour itself out with many a groan and a tear and struggle, before it is in a fit condition of release to hear that ever-speaking voice.

So Jehoshaphat "set himself to seek the Lord", separated himself by fasting from all that would distract, publicly reasoned with God as to why He should help, and with a final admission of helplessness and bewilderment, asked God to work.

The rest now followed just in the way we would expect, resulting in a mighty national exploit of faith. Up arose a prophet who assured the king and people by the word of the Lord that there was no need to fear or fight in this battle; they were just to march out to-morrow, stand still when they came in sight of the enemy, and see the Lord's salvation. (Prophets were God's messengers in those days, because the Spirit and the Word were not yet given to the Church.) But such a word would have been to Jehoshaphat as the voice of one who mocked, if his heart had not been first prepared to take it. By now, by fearing and fasting, reasoning and groaning, the soil was ploughed up ready to receive the seed of faith.

King and people accepted, worshipped, prayed. Then, next morning (what sort of a night does a man have who has already believed in a crisis?), Jehoshaphat spoke out the word of faith. The mountain top was reached. "Hear me, O Judah, and ye inhabitants of Jerusalem; believe in the Lord your God, so shall ye be established; believe His prophets (His Word), so shall ye prosper." And so complete was his faith it had reached the laughing stage, and in place of setting the battle in array, he proposed sending forward a choir! And so intoxicated with faith were the people that they agreed. Was there ever such a marching out to battle?

The end is well known. How, as Judah sang and praised, the three armies got fighting among themselves, till they had completely destroyed each other; and how, when Judah arrived, they found them all "dead bodies fallen to the earth", and it took them three days to gather the spoil.

Upon what did it all hang? Upon Jehoshaphat giving time to get God's mind upon it. Without this, such fantastic behaviour could never have entered the mind of a level-headed ruler. With it, a glorious victory was won without a casualty.

Look at the great crises of faith in the Bible, and the same two facts are constantly outstanding; first, a period of preliminary consultation with God, a staff-meeting away from the firing line; then, a sweeping victory with remarkably small output of energy or loss of life. See Moses at the Red Sea, Joshua at Jordan, Joshua at Jericho, Jonathan and the Philistines, David and Goliath, David at Ziklag, Hezekiah and the Assyrians, Paul and the shipwreck.

Those who would walk in any degree a sure path of faith must learn to do the same. The habit of retirement must be acquired. No matter how busy the life, time must always be found, and can be found, for men will aways find time for what they really want to do. And in that quiet corner each situation must be weighed. We may appear to do the talking and God the listening, as with Jehoshaphat. We may spread the matter before God. We may reason as to why He should act for us. We may search into motives. We may make supplication. But really it is God getting His own mind through to us, the Spirit helping our infirmities, for we know not what to pray for as we ought; until gradually or suddenly assurance is ours.

boldness is ours, heaven is open to us, the throne is a throne of grace, and we are seated with Him in the place of plenty and authority. The Spirit has prayed through us according to the Father's will. The circuit is complete: from the Father to our minds by the Spirit; from our minds back to the Father by the Spirit. The hidden power is released.

Chapter Twenty-Two

UNPRODUCTIVE FAITH

ONE problem of importance remains. What about the baffling occasions when the stand of faith is taken and nothing happens? All people of faith have such experiences, times when either no answer comes, or only a partial one.

A common explanation is to say that God's answer has been "No". This is unsatisfactory. It is not much more than a neat side-step. It is correct on only one condition: that God has actually said "No" to the petitioner, and he knows it. The famous case of this was when Paul asked three times for deliverance from the thorn in his flesh, and God's answer was a refusal. But not a bare negative, far from it, for "all the promises of God are yea". The "refusal" consisted of a revelation to Paul that it is in a man's weakness that God's strength is made perfect; and, seeing this, so far from showing mystification or disappointment, Paul thanked God for the answer and "took pleasure" in his infirmities. An answer indeed, the blessing from which has echoed down through the ages. If God really does say "No", we may always be sure it will be that kind of "No" which is in reality a much greater "Yes".

It is along this line that the solution must be sought for on every occasion of unanswered prayer. First of all, we must hold it as an unassailable corner-stone of our faith that "all the promises of God are yea". We must never let go of that. If baffled, we must just first say with Paul: "Let God be true, though every man be false"; and, with Job: "Though He slay me, yet will I trust in Him." We must stand to it that, even if we should not see the answer till the Day declare it, yet God *has* answered. The one thing which never must fail is our faith which declares His faithfulness.

We must also be on the alert to recognize the answer when it does come. The ways of God are as fresh and varied in grace as in nature. He is always original. He plainly warns us that His ways are not our ways, and it is possible to miss seeing the answer or even to refuse it, because it does not come through the agency or in the manner we expected. God's answers usually come so quietly and naturally that only those who are looking for them can recognize them for what they are. To anyone else they seem ordinary occurrences. This was how Naaman almost missed the healing. Surely the prophet would do something dramatic. But to go and bathe like any common villager in Jordan! And for the message to come through the prophet's servant! Not in wind, earthquake or fire did God speak to Elijah, but by a still small voice. And all those who live in a relationship with God in which answers to prayer are a constant occurrence become accustomed to seeing things just "turn up". Indeed, God will always use the natural, if He can, for He is the God of nature and order. That is why He will not answer a prayer for us which we can answer for ourselves. We must do what lies in our power first, and then we can look to Him to do what we cannot. In numberless instances, men begin to ask God for things, and before long the inner Voice tells them that they are the answer to their own prayers.

It is easy to get into bondage over unanswered prayer. Something must be wrong with the one who is praying. Sin is there, or presumption, or unbelief, or, more commonly still, it is not the will of God. It is a favourite method of the enemy to dishearten, so that we shall give up praying with faith for anything. The answer to all this is: Keep believing. "Fear not, only believe." " 'Tis looking downward that makes one dizzy", as the poet writes. Such is the abounding grace of God that He always has the perfect, positive answer to every prayer, even the wrong prayer, even the mistaken prayer; and to the soul who will wait steadily on Him He will make that answer so plain that he can thank Him fully and be satisfied, even as we have seen Paul do. Only wait long enough. Only ask in faith, nothing wavering, for to such he gives His wisdom liberally and upbraideth not.

Some things, we must remember, are much harder to obtain than others. Material things are the easiest. Jesus said that the daily necessaries of life come to those who trust, without asking for them at all. They are just "added" to those who seek His kingdom first, by the Father who feeds the birds and arrays the flowers, and who all the more certainly knows the needs of His own children before they ask. The provision of material needs, indeed, is, according to Jesus, the fulfilment of a spiritual law. If we give, it is given to us, and so superabundant is the heavenly measure that for our mere moderate giving we receive a return "pressed down and running over". Paul said the same when he reminded the Corinthians that "he that soweth bountifully shall reap also bountifully".

Note also that this return "shall *men* give into our bosom".[1] It is the outworking of an inner spiritual law. Give to men and men give to us. By some means, we know not how, the Spirit moves in men's hearts so that the response to the giver is far greater than the gift he gave. Not, indeed, response from the actual recipient of the gift. The way the Spirit seems to work is that, when we

[1] Luke 6: 38.

receive a gift, we are moved to show our gratitude. Often we cannot in any way recompense the kind donor: it may not be either seemly or possible. But the spirit of recompense is stirred within us and a way opens up to recompense another, really as an act of gratitude to God for the former gift; and thus giving and receiving, receiving and giving, flow on round the world. Giving is really like the circulation of the blood. It comes back to the starting-point. What we give comes back, only in greater abundance. What we hold unnecessarily to ourselves chokes the inflow. Give, to receive, to give again, to receive again, to give again, and so it goes on. All the industrial problems of our day, the inequality of possessions, the poverty, have their ultimate source in the fact that this golden secret was lost in the fall, when grab and keep, in place of give and receive and give again, becomes man's only method of getting provision and security. A simple rule is: if in need, give.

"Life ultimately consists in circulation," writes one: "whether within the physical body of the individual or on the scale of the solar system; and circulation means a continual flowing round; and use of possessions is no exception to this universal law of all life. When once this principle becomes clear to us, we shall see that our attention should be directed rather to the giving than the receiving. We must look upon ourselves, not as misers' chests to be kept locked for our own benefit, but as centres of distribution. If we choke the outlet the current must slacken, and a full and free flow can be obtained only by keeping it open. The generous feeling which is the intuitive recognition of this great law of circulation does not make its first question in any undertaking: How much am I going to *get* by it? But, How much am I going to *do* by it? And making *this* the first question, the getting will flow in with a generous profusion. We are not called upon to give what we have not yet got, and to run into debt; but we are to give liberally of what we have, with the knowledge that by so doing we are setting the law of circulation to work."

To liberate souls by prayer, however, or to move a company to repentance or revival, is a far more difficult task than getting material things. There is an enemy to overcome. The one who spoke to Daniel in a vision after his three weeks' fast said he was prevented from coming for twenty-one days by satanic opposition. There is man's will to be moved. How a free will can be compelled by prayer to make a certain choice, and yet remain free, is a point more of philosophical than practical interest. We know no adequate explanation; but we know that the Bible presents us with the unsolved paradox of God's almightiness and man's free will, and tells us to believe both and act on either as the need arises, and both prove true!

Both these citadels need storming, and the history of the Church is crammed with evidence that only by travail of soul, by prayer and fasting, by a faith that wrestles on towards heaven 'gainst storm and wind and tide, are brands plucked from the burning; by the mother who agonizes through nights and days for her boy, and, when he comes back at last to God, tells him that she always held him fast in her faith and love; by the minister or praying group who seek God's face till they find Him for an outpouring of the Spirit which will melt and fuse and revitalize the Christians, and start a saving work amongst the unconverted. And each such persistent pray-er is but a mirror of that One whose "strong feet", in the classic lyric, *The Hound of Heaven,* "followed, followed after with unhurrying chase and unperturbed pace, deliberate speed, majestic instancy", until at last "the Voice above their beat" was heard by the piteous fleeing soul:

> *That Voice is round me like a bursting sea;*
>   *'And is thy earth so marred,*
>   *Shattered in shard on shard?*
> *Lo, all things fly thee, for thou fliest Me!*
>   *Strange, piteous, futile thing,*
> *Wherefore should any set thee love apart? . . .*
>   *Alack, thou knowest not*
> *How little worthy of any love thou art!*
> *Whom wilt thou find to love ignoble thee*
>   *Save Me, Save only Me?*
> *All which I took from thee I did but take,*
>   *Not for thy harms,*
> *But just that thou might'st seek it in My Arms.*
>   *All which thy child's mistake*
> *Fancies as lost, I have stored for thee at home:*
>   *Rise, clasp My hand, and come!'*
>   *Halts by me that footfall:*
>   *Is my gloom, after all,*
>   *Shade of His Hand, outstretched caressingly?*
>   *'Ah fondest, blindest, weakest,*
>   *I am He Whom thou seekest!*
> *Thou dravest love from thee, who dravest Me!'*[1]

Perhaps the most baffling problem of all in relation to unanswered prayer is the problem of physical healing. We have to face the fact that the responses to living faith recorded in the Bible were nearly always both instantaneous and complete. But that is not so to anything like the same extent in response to present-day faith. Honest investigation shows that, whereas there are genuine cases of faith healing, there are also many hundreds who have prayed

[1] Francis Thompson.

and believed, have been anointed and had hands laid upon them, and there has been no deliverance. There are others, not a few, who have experienced temporary relief, only to see the malady return again after a while.

Yet we have a clear word of Scripture on the subject—nothing could be clearer—in James 5: 15: "and the prayer of faith shall save the sick, and the Lord shall raise him up."

For this we can give no adequate reason, but what we cannot explain we can obey. "The prayer of faith shall save the sick." What does "the prayer of faith" entail? More than asking, supplicating, hoping, as we have already learned. Indeed, this expression "prayer of faith" is plain evidence that there is praying which is not of faith. This qualifying expression implies that what is asked is also received, recognized as one's possession here and now, reckoned on as a present reality. Faith calls the things that be not as though they were.

Apply that now to a need of physical healing, coupled, if it is a help to faith, with the anointing with oil or laying on of hands mentioned here and in other places, for these are merely an outward sign of the inward act of believing. Healing is asked for, healing is received by faith, on the authority of these verses.

What then? Are we to keep looking for the outward manifestation of the healing of the body? Just here may lie our common mistake. If faith means believing we have received, do people keep looking for what they already have? Do they not rather bear witness to their faith by thanksgiving and testimony, and maintain themselves in the attitude of having rather than seeking and expecting?

To receive healing by faith is to reckon on the Spirit of life in Christ Jesus at work in our mortal bodies, and in our souls and spirits. We count on His life, we realize Him as our life. We don't live in a strain, hoping, wondering, doubting. Faith will be a fight in times of physical suffering and weakness, at other times it will be a rest; but we walk by faith, that is all that matters.

And the outcome? The way in which God manifests Himself in response to faith is His affair. Manifest Himself He will, for faith is a law of the spiritual realm. In some, there will be the miraculous healing. In some, and there are very many, the real root of the trouble is not physical at all, but nervous or spiritual. The consequence to these of the steadfast attitude to faith will be to quieten nerves, relieve fear, remove hidden sin and consequent hidden condemnation (James 5: 15, 16). The attention of the sufferer will more and more tend to be centred upon the positive fact of God's life in the body instead of upon negative and destructive mental occupation with the disease. It may often be found that, nerves, mind and heart becoming rested in Him, the symptoms of the disease quickly disappear.

Indeed, many prove that the regular health of the body has been enormously improved since a positive reckoning on the fact of God's life coursing through the physical frame has replaced the old fears, for instance, of cold weather, and infection. Fear, we might almost say, is the first form of disease, and faith the first form of health.

Finally, there are those in whom the answer is not manifested physically. The answer is manifest, but it is "My grace is sufficient for thee; for My strength is made perfect in weakness." The resurrection life of Christ is seen, perhaps, most strikingly of all in spiritual victory over physical suffering; the oppressed becomes the blessed, the one in need of comfort becomes the comforter, the one in need of bedside ministration becomes the shining minister of a triumphing Christ.

Moreover, it must ever be remembered that God has

not promised the redemption of the body in this age. That is for the age to come; a hope of future full deliverance which saves us, Paul says, while we "groan within ourselves, waiting for the adoption, to wit, the redemption of our body". Death, therefore, comes to all, and, in facing the possibility of death in ourselves, or, still more difficult, in our loved ones, we must be sure that we have the fully victorious attitude of faith: that, in spite of human pain and sorrow, we see the glory of being with Christ, we stand ready for that final leap of faith—into sight, into the arms of our Beloved—and we can rejoice when others cross the bar, congratulating them, even as Paul asked the Christians to do for him when he was to be offered as a sacrifice for them. If a loved one is prayed for, even believed for, and is then taken home, faith must burst right through the veil and see the perfect answer in eternity: "On the earth the broken arcs; in the heaven, a perfect round."

It is faith that matters, not the way the answer comes. Faith is the victory, be it manifested in sudden healing, in a new general standard of health, in a victory of spirit within a still-ailing frame, or in triumph over the grave.

Chapter Twenty-Three

A YOUNG Christian leader in the U.S.A., whose life and ministry have been greatly enriched by a fuller understanding of the principles of faith and prayer, wrote to a fellow-worker about the lessons he had been learning. The letter was not meant for publication, and possibly some things in it need qualification; but it glows with the enthusiasm of one who has found great spoil; it is written with the conviction of one who has proved for over five years the truth of what he is saying; and it sums up in personal experience much of what we have written in these recent chapters on guidance and faith in the daily life. As the writer owed some of the light he was given to the teachings outlined in this book, we feel justified in quoting the letter.

"During the past six years," he wrote, "the Lord has led me along rather radical lines when it comes to the matter of prayer and intercession.

"Previous to the coming of X., I had a real hunger in my heart to really get into a life of effective prayer and intercession. And I took various measures to achieve it too. I had read Praying Hyde, David Brainerd, Finney and others. I can well recall several times when I went on whole all-night prayer meetings when certain things were pressing. But somehow the wheels ground so slowly. My hunger for reality intensified and ached. This wasn't the answer! Then came X. with a message on these matters which was so bewildering that I was knocked off my feet.

He spoke of guided prayer, of faith, of the word of authority, of commissions, of life the way Jesus lived it. How different from the way I had been trying to follow. The words rang in my ears. 'Learn of me, for my yoke is easy and my burden is light...' All of this was so new to me that for the next months I was in the greatest perplexity, afraid to pray lest I do it wrong. When we went to see X. the one burden which cried aloud within me was to find out from him the HOW of effective prayer. Three times I asked him. Three times I poured out my heart, faint yet pursuing. And three times he looked at me with a very understanding look (for he had been over the ground himself) and said kindly: 'Keep at it, you'll get there.'

"At first my heart was filled with bitter disappointment. Why didn't he tell me? He knew the answer, then why not help me? It didn't take too long until God showed me that X. had done the wisest thing. There was a unique stroke of spiritual insight and genius in the way he dealt with me. If he had given me an answer, a technique, a method, a ritual, I would have gone home and would have tried to work it for all I was worth. That's what I had done after reading the life of Brainerd and those other fellows. And I would have done it over again... But, by answering me as he did, he threw me off on the Lord, and I had somehow to press through until I found *Him*, and not some method, or technique, or ritual.

"I often think of the story of Christian in *Pilgrim's Progress*. There are very few things which I have read anywhere where I have observed such rich understanding of God's ways. Christian had left the City of Destruction. He had crossed through the Mudhold of Despond. There on the other side he met Evangelist. He began to tell Evangelist his story—of his fleeing the city, of the Slough of Despond, of others who had turned back, and most of all of the great burden on his back. He couldn't stand it any longer. How could he get rid of it? Would Evangelist please tell him? Evangelist knew the answer. He could have told him, but he didn't. Instead he bade the pilgrim look way down the road as far as he could see and said: 'Do you see yonder light?' The pilgrim shaded his eyes and peered through squinted eyes far down the road, and said: 'I think I see it!' Then Evangelist instructed him: 'Go on down the road towards that light until you come to a wicket gate, and on the other side it shall be told thee what thou shalt do...' The Pilgrim wasn't ripe yet! The great need with me and with so many more is not an answer, a technique, a method—but a drastic obedience and steadfastness to whatever measure of light I see, or think I see! And as I go I shall get more light until beyond the wicket gate I meet not a technique, not a ritual, not a sacrament, but Him who alone can remove my load and set me free.

"When that became clear to me, I took a determined step and a radical one. I took my cherished prayer-life which I had nursed and trained and wept over and threw it out of the window. Out went all schedules, times and seasons. I determined that henceforth I would never again try to develop or cultivate a prayer-life. I was no longer interested in a prayer-life as such. I was ready to begin with nothing and to learn the ways of the Lord from scratch as He taught them to me.

"I can't tell you what an immense release came into my soul, and it has since then never departed. At last I felt I was beginning to get to grips with reality. At last I was honest with myself and with God; and, beginning there, I was ready for anything orthodox or unorthodox, which He might lead me into. Right there I began to form the practice of a never-ending waiting upon God, free, restful, natural. From then on I saw the experiences of Brainerd and others like that with new eyes. Up till then I would argue that because men who lived like that and prayed like that were mighty men of God, therefore if I wanted to be a mighty man of God, I should go and do likewise. But not so any more. From then on these men were to me examples of how God had led some men, and they were an encouragement to me to believe that as men sought God, so indeed He would be found of them. 'According to your faith be it unto you.' As one writes: 'Whatsoever ye desire, ye shall have. Those who seek a vision, receive a vision. Those who seek signs receive signs. Those who seek a Christ who manifests Himself as the Author of peace or love, purity or fire, receive as they choose.' Thus I no longer sought to copy the pattern set by these men, and I no longer made any attempt to follow any schedule or method or ritual or form.

"My whole attention began to get turned towards God —full of breathless expectation. I came to see that as His co-worker it was my business to be so open to Him that He could show me His ways, so that my expressional life of prayer or action might be just a simple reflection or manifestation of the will and desire and heart of God as they were breathed into my mind and soul by the Holy Spirit. And, so far, this has taken no set form with me. This was the pattern that Jesus set forth by His life: 'The Son can do nothing of Himself, but what He seeth the Father doing; for what things soever He doeth these the Son doeth in like manner.'

"Since then whenever some preacher fires away at an audience with such thrusts as 'Martin Luther prayed two hours a day, how many hours do you pray? The great sin is the sin of prayerlessness. . . etc.' I am no longer moved by it. It sounds pious and convicting, but to my mind it misses the boat completely. People who are moved by that kind of talk go home and try for all they are worth to pray more and to go round and round that endless mulberry bush of prayer-form, and they get nowhere and get nothing but discouragement and leanness of soul.

"The position to which the Lord brought me also gave me evangelical eyes with which to see the fallacy of much praying of to-day which is of the Old Covenant and under the law. I ran into big patches of it up at a certain Bible School. A lot of fellows came to see me about how to nourish and develop their spiritual lives. I was surprised at their honesty. Dozens of them told me that they felt dry and famished in their spiritual lives. Their testimony was stale. Prayer was uninteresting. They didn't hunger for the things of God the way they wanted. And all kinds of things like that. So I asked them how long this had been going on with them. And with some it had been that way for a long time. Then I asked them what measures they had taken to deal with it and to obtain freshness and vigour and vitality and life. And they told me a tale which I knew so well. They had tried to pray more. They had tried to read the Bible more diligently. They had tried to witness even when they had really nothing to say in the hope that by doing something like that they would somehow be returned into the green pastures. Some had confessed sins in the meetings. Some had fasted. And I can't tell you all that they had done. They had tried methods, techniques, prayer-rituals, forms of resisting, standing, sitting, binding, loosing, etc., and they were all worn out.

"So I asked each one very simply: 'How did you get saved? By reading the Bible, by praying, by *doing anything?*' Never! No one ever got saved that way. Not by the works of the law. No man is ever justified that way. But by simple faith, simple believing, simple receiving. So I told them: 'As therefore ye received Christ Jesus the Lord, so walk in Him.' It's as simple as that. They had begun in the Spirit but were seeking to maintain that life and to perfect it in the flesh. Nice, good, religious, pious, earnest, zealous—but flesh all the same. Self-effort. How often men preach that, if you don't want to lose out with God, you have to read the Bible and pray and do all kinds of things. We get a stack of magazines here from all kinds of societies. It's common to see this idea held out that finances don't come in, souls aren't saved, workers don't offer themselves, and in general thing aren't getting on too well because—well, because we aren't praying enough, we aren't doing this, that or the other thing enough. Brother, that's the Old Covenant, that's under the law, that's setting about to perfect in the flesh that which was perhaps begun in the Spirit. My whole soul stands up and cries 'No, no, a thousand times no!' The roots of the trouble go deeper than that. You can't make a tree good by pinning on a few more branches. Such an emphasis misses the boat completely! Dryness, dullness, lack of supply, failure and all these things are merely the symptoms of inner disease. You cannot remedy the disease by treating the symptoms. A lack of freedom in prayer and loss of hunger for the Word and such like things simply indicate that at bottom something is wrong. And that wrong will never be touched by somehow trying to pray more or read the Word more, or any such thing, never!

"For these reasons I don't feel that it is at all my business to go around and encourage people to pray, or to tell them how to carry on heavenly business on behalf of the work of God abroad. That's not the focal point that needs emphasis. The people are exhorted to death already. Preachers exhort and exhort and exhort, drive and drive, instruct and instruct.

"But I can and do try to do a few things: 1. I feel that I can give information concerning God's job. And this covers a lot; its purpose, scope, dimensions, oppositions, enemies, objectives and many other things. 2. I can set forth clearly the personal obligations of God's people towards this information. 3. I can encourage them to wait upon the Lord with open hearts to find out what He wants them to do about it. 4. I can urge them and encourage them to obey what they are told, and help a little in instructing those who are obedient as to how they can best do what they are told.

'The chief point to get at is that of basic relationship to God. When that is wrong, then all these ills of which we have been speaking naturally follow. But when that relationship is right, then the Holy Spirit will have a chance to have His way and lead them to go abroad, or to take up some commission here at home, or to give themselves to intercession, or to take up a programme of heavenly labours such as Brainerd went through, or whatever it may be. That's God's business to lead them into whatever He likes.

"A great point in some societies is that of gathering up a filing-index of folks who pledge themselves to pray for the workers who go. I have seen this practice so much abused that I am fearful of it. In so many missions it just becomes a neat way of lining up a list of supporters. And then if things are not going so well, they very conveniently blame the list of pray-ers and plead with them not to let them down. There is a fearful danger in this.

"Carey's illustration: 'I go yonder to dig, you folks at home must hold the ropes,' is very touching and appealing, but is also dangerous. It is dangerous to the fellow who goes to dig, in the first place. He can get to be too occupied with the rope and with the folks at the other end who hold it. Then, if the rope breaks or if the folks let go at the other end, he is sunk.

"When Jesus commissioned the disciples He sent them forward with the promise—not of people holding the ropes, but with His own personal presence. 'Lo, I am with you always.' That seemed to be sufficient. When Paul set out he never seemed to look back to either Antioch or Jerusalem to feel whether the folks back there were still holding the ropes. I know that in his epistles he asks the folks to remember him in prayer that doors may be open to him, or that he may have boldness in preaching. But these folks were his converts, they were the folks on his mission field, not the folks back home who somehow or other were supposed to be holding the ropes for him as he went out in their name on their behalf.

"The snare is to get eyes off of God and on to men, and when one does, the game is up.

"Then, in the second place, there is a snare in that holding the ropes illustration (which is not a Scriptural illustration), as far as the people are concerned who are supposed to be at home holding the ropes. From as far back as I can remember the punchless challenge at the end of almost every missionary presentation is a very sickly and pathetic directive. 'Of course we all can't go to meet these awful needs, but we can at least pray and give some money.' That takes the teeth out of Christ's command and His lordship over their lives. And thousands of people are obeying the Lord's command by proxy, through some fellow or girl who has gone as their representative and through whom, as they pray for them and give for their support, they feel that they themselves are going in obedience. And thus their conscience gets a rest while they sit in disobedience.

"The note that must be struck, and struck hard, is the note of Christ's right to have lordship over their lives. His command is to go. Folks had better go to Him and find out what His orders are for them specifically. If it is to go, then they had better not stay around and pray. If it is to give, then they had better not substitute intercession. If it is to intercede, then they cannot obey by just putting money in the plate. If we go preaching to folks the necessity of becoming intercessors, then I feel that we are missing the chief point and will be laying burdens on people which the Holy Spirit is not laying. But if they will face up to the will of the Holy Spirit, then I dare to say that God will raise up such folks to be intercessors as He shall deem necessary. For folks on the fields to get occupied with burdens to pray that intercessors be raised up at home, is to get tangled up with burdens which they could afford to leave well alone. God will care for such needs here, just as He will take care to see that financial supporters are raised up.

"To sum up this point, let me point out the simple relationship which characterized Paul's tie-up with the home base. Acts 14: 26 tells of Paul's return to Antioch: 'from whence they had been committed to the grace of God for the work which they had fulfilled.' And in 15:40 Paul chose Silas and then began another journey: 'and they went forth (from Antioch), being commended by the brethren to the grace of the Lord.' There wasn't much else that the brethren could do. They were persuaded that God was able to guard these men whom they had committed to His grace.

"That which will sustain you clear through, even in the deepest waters, will be only the presence of Christ.

'Though I go through the valley of the shadow of death, I will fear no evil, for THOU ART WITH ME!' It would be fatal at such times to lean on anything less than the presence of the Lord. The Holy Spirit will cause other people to pray, but the fellow in the front trench would do better to keep his mind on the Lord alone! and not on people, even if they are praying people.

"The heavenly life is not 'up there' somewhere. It is no higher than the floor you walk on. Jesus said it was better for us if He should go up to heaven because then He would send the Holy Spirit *down here* to enable us to get the job done. So while He is looking after our affairs 'up there', He has left it up to the Holy Spirit and us to look after His affairs *down here*. Let's be careful that we don't get caught in the false business of somehow trying to get into the heavenlies, 'that is to bring Christ down'. But the 'righteousness which is of faith saith: the word is nigh thee, in thy mouth and in thy heart; that is, the word of faith which we preach.'

"That which gives the warrior power for the job down here is not getting all occupied with all kinds of things way up somewhere 'in the heavenlies'. But Jesus promised that we would have all the power we needed, and protection and authority, and healing, and guidance and victory over every enemy by a personal union with the Holy Spirit. He alone is authorized to minister to us the things of Christ, and He has been sent to do that for us down here. As He dwells within me down here He shall minister to me power and authority to tread upon serpents and scorpions and *over all the power of the enemy,* and nothing shall in any wise hurt me!

"Now I am all for simply taking that just as it stands and believing it. I don't see where it is said that this shall be so IF day by day, morning and evening, you diligently go through a ritual of binding and loosing, withstanding, resisting, etc., up in some imagined heavenly realm. But this will be true day or night, rain or shine, in the man who in simple faith trusts the Holy Spirit to maintain His rule and authority in his inner heart and disposition, perpetually, all the time, whether he is praying or not. Then whatever praying he does, or praising, or resisting, etc., it will be simply the outward expression of his inner state of being, and such expressions will not be a means by which he seeks to attain to a position of authority, or to maintain his freedom in God, or to achieve victory over obstacles. Not at all.

"Now, Satan can attack me on these outward things. He can throw me into jail or make my horse fall down, or he can throw darkness and depression and dryness and oppression over me. He can make me feel dull and hopeless and weak. He can buffet me, roar at me, sacre me, and make praying almost impossible for me. But he cannot touch my inner relationship to the Lord, my union with the Holy Spirit, my certain assurance of victory. Not at all. Though we be pressed on every side, we are not straitened. Though he makes us perplexed, yet he cannot make us despair. Though he pursues us, yet we are not forsaken. Though he smites us down, yet he cannot destroy us.

"But, you say, what about those times when the devil oppresses you so much that you cannot pray, can't carry out various heavenly labours? What shall you do then? My answer would be; just stand still. Don't do anything. By all means don't go whacking at him. You only invite a fight. It takes two to make a fight, and if you don't fight, then there won't be any. As long as you just stand still and refuse to be taken up with anything other than your position of union with the Lord Jesus, he can't do more than growl and throw sand in your face. Luther suggests that you just laugh at him, for if he refuses to depart when presented with the Scripture, then he will soon leave when you laugh at him, for he can't stand that scorn. And, by the way, the Bible says that such laughing is a real part of the heavenly 'labours' too. Psalm 2 says that when all the kings set themselves against the Lord and against His anointed servants, then 'He that sitteth in the heavens will laugh: the Lord will have them in derision.' And the Scripture affirms that we are seated with Him in the heavens, so let's laugh with Him. If that's heavenly 'labours', then lead me to it!

"If it gets tough to pray, then quit trying to pray any more. He can touch your form but not your inner relationship and position. And just because you stop your ritual it doesn't mean that you have altered your position of faith and authority one whit. It's not your going through the ritual that's going to defeat him and give you the land. It's your inner attitude of faith, and that he cannot touch, even though he padlock your mouth and fill your body with fear so that you can't even think to pray.

"It is far more important that you just rest quietly in God and not be moved in spirit than that you go through some kind of prayer-ritual. Where he fools us and gets us is when he gets us all in a stew and under a burden and even into a feeling of condemnation, because we find it so hard to pray and feel that however tough it is we must go through our outward form and ritual of heavenly 'labours' of intercession and such like. . . No, just quit trying. After that you have suffered awhile the Lord will bruise Satan under your feet. He will flee from you when you resist him without force and without taking note of him. And then the Holy Spirit will again gently lead you to pray or sing or praise or anything else by which you can most easily and naturally express the faith that is in you and the position and relationship which you enjoy with God, a relationship which has passed untouched and unscathed through the worst of the devil's assaults. It is the basic faith and relationship which wins the day and wins in the end. God will let the devil douse you again and again, that your basic faith and union with Him may be proved and found perfect at the day of His coming. For that inner faith and disposition is to Him more precious than silver or gold.

"Take a look at Paul. After he had been up in the third heaven he says that there was given to him a thorn in the flesh, *a messenger from Satan to buffet him* that he should not be exalted overmuch. Three times he asked the Lord that it might be removed, but the Lord told him that it was good for him. So Paul embraced it, embraced the messenger of Satan! And you know how the rest of that passage goes. Thus God uses the devil to polish up His saints and makes them strong in Christ's power.

"See how this was likewise true in the life of Christ. After His baptism, where He had been anointed with the power of the Holy Spirit for His ministry, it says that immediately He was led by the Holy Spirit into the wilderness be be assailed by the devil. That was arranged by God and directed by the Holy Spirit. And when He had had enough, His Father had the angels right there to minister unto Him. Because He has suffered being tempted, He is able to succour them which are tempted or tested. See how, for over three years, He was able to escape the devil's attacks by the simple declaration that the hour had not yet come. And when the hour came He took all that was coming, forbidding Peter to do anything to defend Him. Under God's permission it was now the devil's hour. And the awful hellish brew which the devil handed Him in the cup of suffering He took, embraced it as coming from the Father's hand, and drank it to the dregs. Satan stripped Him, hung Him out in open shame, and killed Him; but he could not touch the basic inner relationship which He had to the Father and the faith which He had that the Father would see Him through to resurrection ground.

"And, lastly, I think of James 1: 'Count it all joy, my brethren, when you fall into manifold temptations and trials, knowing that the proving of your faith worketh steadfastness; and let steadfastness have its perfect work, that ye may be perfect and entire, lacking in nothing.'

"Here is set down with unmistakable language just what ought to be our attitude towards the hardships and trials and temptations which come our way. The negative is refuted by the positive. Light swallows up darkness. Evil is overcome by good. The devil's assaults are the meat and drink of steadfastness and patient faith. That leaflet 'The Adventure of Adversity' goes a step farther and shows how these very assaults in the grasp of faith become redemptive, and can be the very instruments by which we can achieve our desired ends."

Chapter Twenty-Four

HARMONIOUS RELATIONSHIPS

(i) With Things

LIFE is response to environment, and man's environment
is on three levels, spiritual, social, material. Harmonious living means that man has learned the way of
right relationships with God, with people, with things.
Now, a relationship implies a recognition of mutual rights,
both sides in a relationship have a life of their own and
a standing of their own, which demands respect and freedom of expression; and the relationship must be a right
adjustment between them, a working agreement which
gives full and happy scope for both in a unity of purpose
and action. Therefore, a relationship is a living bond between living beings. It cannot properly be said that there
is a relationship between a possessor and a thing possessed.
There is a connection, that is all. The one uses, arranges,
experiences the other, but there is no life in the experience, no fellowship, no inter-communion, no give and
take.

But we said above that right living is learning the way
of right relationships with God, with people, and with
things. That is just the point. The spiritual mind is relationship and life, but the carnal mind, connection and
death.

What is the attitude of the natural man, infected with
"all that is in the world, the lust of the flesh, and the lust
of the eyes and the pride of life"? Is it not to possess all
people and things, and even God Himself, for his own

convenience? He would use religion, friends, material possessions, all alike as his ladder to security and success. Even his prayers are, according to James, asking for things that he may consume them on his own lusts. Even as he would dare to "possess" God, if he could, so he will try to "possess" man; whether it be a Caesar of old time and his slaves, a Sultan and his harem, or the modern totalitarian state and its conscripts. Such is the essence of the fall, the rejection of a living relationship with God and His created world, and the substitution of the greed and grab of possession, which is merely a dead connection.

Inherent, therefore, in the new creation in Christ is a new three-fold relationship: as Paul said, a life lived not unto ourselves, but unto *Christ;* and the knowing henceforth of no *man* after the flesh; and a passing away of old *things,* all things becoming new:[1] the new relationship to God and men and things.

The emphasis now is on relationship. Life is fellowship. Man was originally created for fellowship. Man was re-created for fellowship "with the Father and with His Son Jesus Christ". God Himself founded His creation for the purpose of relationship, not connection, when He made man in His own image; not an automaton He could command, but a being whom He Himself could not coerce but only persuade, and on whose reclamation He expended all the riches of His wisdom, so that He might find a way of transforming determined enemies into loving sons.

This new life of relationship, in its first form of fellowship with God, we have been examining in earlier chapters. In its second form, of fellowship with man, much is involved, much that touches family, business, church and

[1] 2 Cor. 5: 15-17.

national life; social, economic and political questions; class, colour, and sex problems. To these we shall give some attention now. But before we do so, for a few moments we will look at the third form, the new relationship with things. In what sense can it ever be said that we have more than a connection with things? How can we have a relationship with them?

In this sense. While all things are held fast by us in the closed circuit of our self-life, chattels for our use, we can only see them from that point of view. They are merely conveniences, food to eat, powers to harness, materials to mould, beauties to enjoy. Even animal life, if for convenience we include it for the moment under the category of "things", the natural man looks upon as valuable for food and clothing, for burden bearing, for sport, or as vermin to be destroyed; for all know the kind of treatment meted out to animals in lands where Christianity has not spread its influences. The crude and cruel forms of such treatment are even still to be seen in countries with a thousand years of Christian teaching, in our zoos, our shooting-parties, our fox and stag hunting; although it is certainly also true that a regard for animals, a sense of their rights, the realization of a living fellowship with them in place of a mere soulless connection, has now been recognized, even by law, in the life of some peoples.

But when the new light in Christ has dawned, there is a sense in which all things are seen in Him and He is the life of all. They are no longer just "things". They are His creatures, they stretch out invisible hands to us. For even science now reveals to us that "it is not we who are looking out upon nature, but nature which is ever trying to enter and come into touch with us through our senses. If we analyse our sense of sight, we find that the only impression made upon our bodies by external objects is the

image formed upon the retina; we have no cognizance of
the separate electro-magnetic rills forming that image,
which, reflected from all parts of an object, fall upon the
eye at different angles constituting form, and with different frequencies giving colour to that image; that image is
only formed when we turn our eyes in the right direction
to allow those rills to enter; and, whereas those rills are
incessantly beating on the outside of our sense organ
when the eyelid is closed, they can make no impression
unless we allow them to enter by raising that shutter. It is
not then any volition from within that goes out to seize
upon and grasp the truths from nature, but the phen-
omena are as it were forcing their way into our consciousness."[1] God's life is in them, His beauty shines through
them. "Something lives in every hue Christless eyes have
never seen." They are all forms of His love. We use and
experience them as before, but with a new reverence, a
new care. It may yet be proved that our attitude to an
object actually affects it. "Believe in the simple magic of
life, in service in the universe, and the meaning of that
waiting, that alertness, that 'craning of the neck' in
creatures will dawn upon you", writes Martin Buber.[2]
Whether that be so, or no, as a true mechanic feels a relationship with his machine, a good driver with his car, so
a Christian gradually learns to regard the whole of God's
creation. The world is His temple, all objects in it are
sacramental. The whole earth is full of His glory. The
Christian is always worshipping, always praising. The

[1] Sydney Klein, *Science and the Infinite*, pp. 4-5.
[2] In, *I and Thou*, a little book which "is exercising an influence quite
out of proportion to its slender size... and will rank as one of the
epoch-making books for our generation.... Buber gives intellectual
status to the problem of the relation between persons; and has called in
doubt the massive monistic system within which idealistic philosophy
has worked."

very humblest objects of daily use, of the bedroom, of the kitchen, teach lessons of faithful service. He sees with the eyes of the Saviour to whom the beauty of the lily was the Father's adorning, and the common sparrow the Father's little feathered creature: to whom the sun and the rain, the seed and the pearl, the vine and the fig tree, were all the Father's bountiful gifts. And the songs of the poets find an echo in his heart. As Browning, in *Saul:*

I but open my eyes and perfection, no more and no less,
In the kind I imagined, full-fronts me, and God is seen God
In the star, in the stone, in the flesh, in the soul and the clod.
And thus looking within and around me, I ever renew
(With that stoop of the soul which in bending upraises it
too)
The submission of man's nothing-perfect to God's All-
Complete,
As by each new obeisance in spirit, I climb to His feet!

And Mrs. Browning, in *Aurora Leigh:*

Earth's crammed with heaven,
And every common bush afire with God;
But only he who sees, takes off his shoes,
The rest sit round it and pluck blackberries.

Or Tennyson, in his little Sonnet, *Flower in the Crannied Wall:*

Little flower—but if I could understand
What you are, root and all, and all in all,
I should know what God and man is.

And Thomas Edward Brown, in *My Garden:*

A Garden is a lovesome thing, God wot!
Rose Plot,
Fringed pool,

Ferned grot—
The veriest school
of peace; and yet the fool
Contends that God is not—
Not God! in gardens! when the eve is cool?
Nay; but I have a sign;
'Tis very sure God walks in mine.

Or Wordsworth, who "felt the sentiment of Being spread o'er all that moves and all that seemeth still" and wrote in the famous lines on *Tintern Abbey:*

A sense sublime
Of something far more deeply interfused,
Whose dwelling is the light of setting suns,
And the round ocean and the living air,
And the blue sky, and in the mind of man:
A motion and a spirit, that impels
All thinking things, all objects of all thought,
And rolls through all things.

Or Francis Thompson, in *The Mistress of Vision:*

When to the new eyes of thee
All things by immortal power
 Near and far,
 Hiddenly,
To each other linked are,
That thou canst not stir a flower
With troubling of a star...
Seek no more. O seek no more!

And, again in *The Kingdom of God.*

O world invisible, we view thee,
O world intangible, we touch thee,
O world unknowable, we know thee,
Inapprehensible, we clutch thee!

Does the fish soar to find the ocean,
The eagle plunge to find the air—
That we ask of the stars in motion
If they have rumour of thee there?

Not where the wheeling systems darken,
And our benumbed conceiving soars!
The drift of pinions, would we hearken,
Beats at our own clay-shuttered doors.

The angels keep their ancient places;
Turn but a stone, and start a wing!
'Tis ye, 'tis your estranged faces,
That miss the many-splendoured thing.

Even "things", then, take on a new relationship. Faith and love enter and forge a new bond with them. They are still our willing servants. Still "things" to be used. We do not fall into the error of the pantheist, who worships the creature as though it were the Creator; but equally we do not hold the gifts of God in light esteem, not even giving thanks at the meal table, using and abusing them as though life consisted in the abundance of things we possess. Rather, in "having nothing" in the old sense of claiming and holding things as our very own, we find that we "possess all"; all things are ours in the faith and love relationship, as we are Christ's, and He is God's.

Chapter Twenty-Five

HARMONIOUS RELATIONSHIPS

(ii) With People

THE question of our relationships with people is so important that we think it is worth a most careful examination. There is nothing upon which we Christians put more emphasis than on the need of unity. There is nothing that we are quicker to deplore than examples of division. Yet the fact is that to live in free, open, happy relationships with others is an achievement of the highest spiritual order; and those who have dug down to the bottom of the subject, who have thoroughly examined and learned the technique of brotherly love (for there is a technique), and who can apply it on all occasions, are all too few.

Let us get this point clear. We have seen that there are spiritual laws which govern all phases of the Christian life, and that they are discoverable from the Scriptures and applicable to our every condition. We have exhaustively investigated the laws of faith, as they are related to the supply of need, to our relationship with God, to our individual circumstances, to our sphere of service (and let us not be afraid of this word "law", for it is only the term we use to describe some segment of the unsearchable wisdom of God which He has been pleased to reveal, and which man then grasps, labels "law" for convenience, and proceeds to use. "All's love, yet all's law!") And now in the same way, we want to examine the law which governs the exercise of brotherly love on every occasion.

We shall find that is it only another application of the same law of faith. We have seen the way by which the tangles of our self-governed life can be exchanged for the blessings of Christ-control, and the challenge of frustrating circumstances can be turned into the adventure of believing God. It can be the same with the set-backs of inharmonious relationships.

We will take the simplest and most obvious instance. There is someone we have difficulty to get on with. There are clashes. One rubs up the other. Mannerisms, petty selfishnesses, annoying habits; too self-assertive or too self-effacing; too tidy or too slovenly; too cheerful or too mournful; too critical or too gullible. We all know the sort of thing in a thousand different garbs. None can live with others without it happening.

What is to be done about it? Temperaments just do clash, as much as colours. Strive as we may, the opposition rises in us, the criticism, the resentment, the heated words, the strain, the shame at our failures.

Let us look back a moment. If the same law of faith solves our problem, how did it work when we were up against a difficult circumstance rather than person? We learned first to recognize that we are human and have human reactions. We fear, feel helpless, or bewildered, and so on. We then learned, not to come under false condemnation as if such reactions were sinful, but to see that we directed them aright; up, not down; not to give way to doubt and depression, or in other words, to accept the devil's interpretation of the situation, but to find out God's point of view.

That, we then learned, took some effort to discover, an effort in equal proportion to the weight of the pressure on our spirits. We have to go apart deliberately into the secret place and there, by prayer, by reading of the Word, by consideration of the circumstances, rid ourselves of the earthly outlook on the thing and replace it by the heavenly. See it as God sees it. See it from the throne where we sit with Christ. See it in the light of all the power given to Him and to us in Him. Finally we act on that heavenly vision. We speak the authoritative word of faith. "Be gone", or "Come", in Christ's Name, as the case may be. We then go out from the secret place to live in the faith of that declaration and act accordingly. Oftentimes we may feel our weakness all over again, and oftentimes retire again within ourselves to repeat that word of faith and take fast hold of God; but by His grace we persist until one day, maybe as quietly as the evening dew, the thing happens according as we believed.

Apply that now to a difficult person as to a difficult circumstance. Repeat the process stage by stage. Recognize frankly the unpleasant feelings. Do not be condemned by them, just recognize that that person has that effect upon you (and you may be sure that you have that same effect on him). It is just a question of human temperaments. But recognize also that this is the earthly point of view: it is how *you* see your neighbour and how this or that about him rubs *you* up the wrong way; and you must not remain in that point of view, for, by ourselves, we are the helpless prey of the devil.

Now use the same process. Go a step further. Go to the secret place, spread the matter before the Lord, not so much to pray and groan for deliverance, perhaps you have often done that; go to get His point of view on your neighbour, even as you get His point of view on a difficult situation. What does He say or think about him? Ah, that takes on a different aspect. For God does not see us all clothed in our pettinesses, in those little selfishnesses and idiosyncracies which annoy. He sees us in Christ and

Christ in us. He sees His Beloved Son and us in Him. Now that makes all the difference. We look again at our neighbour. We see Christ in that life (supposing him to be the Lord's). We see the changes Christ has wrought. We praise and love, for Christ in us unites with Christ in him. It does not mean that the faults are not there, but it means that the greater fills our vision and the lesser retires to its proper place; for nearly all disunity comes through magnifying the lesser and minimizing the greater in a person.

Now we go out to begin again. By God's grace we are going to reckon on Christ in our brother, rather than see the flesh or even the weak human. But that means something else of great importance. We said that brotherly love is a process of faith. It is. Real love means faith, means we *trust* our brother. Let us test our love by that. How often we will say: "Of course we love so and so, but, but, but...", and out will come all the reasons why we could not trust him. But real love is trust. God even trusted that fallen sinners could and would respond to Christ. There was a sense in which He reckoned on the response of a wicked world or He could not have died for it. And if we cannot trust even a brother in Christ, we can always trust Christ in him; and we can remember that God trusts him and has long patience with him, even as He has with us.

Now, faith is potent. What we believe in we are producing and propagating. Our very looks, words and actions are always propagating our faith. We are always ministering either faith or unbelief, life or death, Christ or devil, every minute of the day. One or the other streams from us. No man lives unto himself. Therefore, if we are reckoning on and believing in a brother's weak point, we are actually strengthening these things in him. If, on the other hand, we are reckoning on Christ in him, we are building up the image of God in him. Therefore our attitude to our brother not only affects us and gives us either release or strain, either bondage or liberty, but it affects him; and we are responsible to God for the way we affect our brother.

Victory may by no means come in a moment. Even as in the battle of faith over a difficult situation, we have to hold the ramparts of faith against many an assault of unbelief and stand fast, so in the battle for brotherly love. We may fall back again and again before an assault of criticism or annoyance or resentful feeling. Well, return again and again to the place of love and faith which sees Christ in him.

The best action to take and the most costly, and therefore most effective, is to tell our brother frankly of the facts of the situation and of God's dealings with us. We shall get nowhere if we merely heatedly tell him where he rubs us up or appears to us to fail. We must involve ourselves also in the statement, by admitting our resentful reactions. That is the approach by the way of the Cross, not telling him to die on it, while we sit and watch him; but dying ourselves first by confessing where we have been wounded and hurt and hard. That will certainly bring a relief and a release to us. Frankness always liberates; and in many cases, such an approach, combining confession with faithfulness, will open the way to a frank talk and honest solution of the problem, or at least a spirit of openness by which the subject can be frankly re-discussed when it re-arises.

To see Christ in him is the solution, there is no other; and even if he does not respond, love then will flow freely in one's own soul. And even if my neighbour is not a child of God, the same principle is valid, for if I cannot see him as one who has Christ in him, I can see him as one whom Christ seeks, and at whose heart's door he is knocking, and in that sense I can see him as Christ sees him, as one He would save.

But now another question arises. This procedure may be feasible when no intentional wrong is done us by our neighbour, when the discord is rather more temperamental than deliberate. But what of the many instances when some real wrong is the cause, some unguarded or malicious statement, some unkind or obstructive act, something that really hurts me or a dear one, and stirs indignation or calls for retribution and rebuke?

Let us remember the one golden rule. Every battle of life is fought and won *within* ourselves, not without. Gain the inner spiritual victory, and the outer follows as sure as the day the night. How hard it is for us to learn that we control and conquer from within. We are used to dealing with the outward, with things and people, and we fly to the outward for supply; wrestle against the outward in adversity, cry out against the outward when wronged. Poor blinded creatures, scratching about for the bits and pieces on the outside, when all the wealth and power of the universe streams into us through the Creator, and He is to be found where spirit meets with Spirit—within!

Who were the poised and powerful among the twelve spies whom Moses sent out? Were they the ten who were influenced by the outward, by the giants and walled cities of Canaan, and who cried out on their return: "We be not able to go up against the people, for they are stronger than we... It is a land that eateth up the inhabitants thereof?" Or the two, Caleb and Joshua, from their standpoint of inner vision and victory, whose minds were stayed on God and who said: "Let us go up at once, and possess it; for we are well able to overcome it... neither

fear ye the people of the land; for they are bread for us?"
Who proved right?

David had a profound and unusual insight into this
truth when meeting with a sudden gross and public in-
sult. When sorrowfully leaving Jerusalem with his company of loyal supporters at the time of Absolom's revolt,
he was accosted by a relative of King Saul's, who cursed
and stoned him. "Come out, come out, thou bloody man,
thou son of Belial: the Lord hath returned upon thee all
the blood of the house of Saul..." This was too much
for one of David's chief officers, Abishai, who drew his
sword and asked permission to kill him: "Why should
this dead dog curse my lord the king? Let me go over, I
pray thee, and take off his head." A convenient way out
of our difficulties which we often feel like taking! David's
answer was remarkable: "What have I to do with you, ye
sons of Zeruiah? So let him curse, because the Lord hath
said unto him: Curse David." And then a little later: "Let
him alone, and let him curse; for the Lord hath bidden
him." And then a quick rise in faith: "It may be that the
Lord will requite me good for his cursing." A man who
is a mouthpiece of the devil was said by David to be
commanded to curse by the Lord! Truly a lightning transition of outlook from the natural reaction of Abishai's
"Kill him", to the supernatural one of David's "Let him
alone, the Lord hath bidden him"; a transition possible
only to one who was long accustomed to walk with God.
The underlying principle is plain to see: a difference of
inner attitude affecting outer action. One saw the thing
from an earth-level, the other the same thing from
heaven.

So in every case of wrong done. There is a way of
peace, poise and victory. But it is not found on the outside by leaping to condemn the wrongdoer and to assert

our own rights. Once again it is by the application on the inside of the one process of faith. Here the fight will be much fiercer. Our sense of righteousness will have been aroused. We have been wronged. The fault is obvious. The wrongdoer should be made to see his wrong and apologize. The wronged one should have his character cleared. It is not even morally sound that the wrongdoer should get away with it unrebuked, unrepentant. He should be shown that sin is sin.

Yes, that is true of the plane of righteousness pure and simple. It is equitable for the man of the world. It is the justice of the law. But, in the Gospel, a new principle of action has been revealed, revolutionary, dazzling. "The meek shall inherit the earth." So quietly said that the world passes it by as one of those "soft" sayings of Christianity. Yet it contains the only explosive power which could blow war out of world policies, and, as it says, will and does inherit the earth.

It is the Cross in action; and Jesus, who fulfilled it, has been gaining His promised inheritance of millions of human hearts through two thousand years, and will one day rule, as prophecy assures us, in person over the whole redeemed earth.

We say to our injurious neighbour, as Abishai said: "*You* must die! If you will die, die by repenting, confessing, apologizing, righting the wrong, then I will freely forgive." But that is just what God in Christ did not do. If He had, we should all be bound for a lost eternity. That is the way of the law.

But God, in face of man's defiances, disobediences, ragings, insults, mockeries, decides that *He* will die in the Person of His Son for us. Christ dies at the hands of wicked men, our hands. Gods loves on. He even becomes our suppliant and beseeches us to make it up with Him.

He, the offended One, does not remain in cold isolation till we make some approach to Him. He comes to us. He breaks through the barriers that separate us. He becomes flesh to reach us. "What more can I do than I have done?" is His own heart's cry through the mouth of the prophet.

And the consequence? Melted human hearts. Men and women by the thousand who will spill their blood for love of His Name. Treasures poured at His feet in endless abundance; treasures of brain and substance, treasures of loved ones and life itself. A very world in darkness and distortion that still through twenty centuries stretches out its suppliant hands to Calvary, recognizing the glory of that bleeding Figure, glimpsing the secret of its power, knowing it holds the only key to effective brotherhood, yet not willing to pay the price of that narrow way.

But to us, His disciples, the challenge comes right home, right to these practical situations of our daily contacts. Can *we* die when our brother offends us, or shall we insist that *he* does? Shall we take that same despised way which leads to real power through seeming weakness, or the apparently sensible way that really leads to weakness through seeming power? The way that conquers him by first being conquered ourselves, or that tries the hopeless task of forcing him to his knees by outward compulsion issuing from the inner weakness of our uncrucified selves?

It is not easy. The spirit is stirred to righteous indignation. Real bitterness is felt maybe, or resentment, or a strong sense of a wrong that should be righted. To retaliate would give relief, to write the strongly worded letter, to take decisive action, to resign or dismiss as the case might be, or to take the case before others for just judgment.

But just a moment. Give God a chance. "Be ye angry", but "sin not". Let Him speak first. And what does He say? Is it not always the same? "I only work through death and resurrection. What about your natural self? Are you not very much alive with resentment and indignation? Have you not sin in that respect, even if your opponent has in other respects? I will deal with you first. Will you die out to yourself?" You respond. You know it is His voice. You consent. By faith you reckon yourself once again as dead and buried with Christ, the sin under the blood.

And now He speaks again. "What about your attitude to your brother? Honest now! Do you see Me in him just now? Do you recognize him as My child whom I love, and does your heart warm to him as a consequence? Or is his fault so magnified in your sight that these other greater facts about him are forgotten?"

Probably it is so, almost certainly so. Well then, reverse the outlook. See him from Christ's point of view. Honour him as one in whom Christ dwells. Count on Christ to work His will in him and to adjust what is wrong.

Ah, now the viewpoint will change. We shall find that a great deal of our resentment was hurt self, not just simply honest indignation at a wrong done. It was because he wronged *me* that I felt like that. We wanted to retaliate because we wanted to relieve our damaged feelings; self lay at the root of most of it, and we may always be sure that to act in the flesh only brings response from the flesh.

Now we can see clearly. Self is exposed in ourselves and dealt with at the Cross. Christ reigns again within, and what we now want is not just our rights with our brother, but that he may be blessed and that God may have His best in him. Now we are in a fit condition to act as God directs. Perhaps it may be a word spoken or letter written, but the tone of the letter will be as much admitting our own failure as his: or maybe silence and faith will be the way. But assurance and peace will be in our hearts, and of this we may be certain, that "the meek inherit", and resurrection life will follow death, life not merely in us but in him, for the one who wins within commands without.

Chapter Twenty-Six

THE UNDERLYING LAW OF FRUITBEARING FAITH

THE life in the Spirit is bound to have one hall-mark—
that the nature of God is reproduced in the personality
handed over to Him; for such a handing-over implies total
immersion in and possession by the Spirit of God, to be
made like Himself, and He is God. God's nature has one
essential characteristic. He is totally self-giving. He pours
Himself out in an everlasting stream of blessing on all
His creation. He is "the eternal will to all goodness". He
finds Himself in losing Himself.

Now, if that Spirit indwells me, He must of necessity
turn me in a like direction. The Spirit that took the
Saviour to Calvary for the world and "drove" Him to
offer Himself without spot unto God, must drive me out
of self-pleasing into self-giving, out of indulgence into
sacrifice, out of security into service, out of care of myself
into concern for others.

This "drive" incidentally, is the glory of the Gospel.
It means that we do not tell the unwilling, the fearful, the
self-pleasing, the soft, which we all are by nature, to be
this or that for God; to deny themselves, to give up things,
to endure hardship, which they cannot and don't want to
do; but we bid them only to do one thing, acknowledging
frankly all weakness and unwillingness—to commit themselves to the control of God's Spirit. That is all. They
need not even necessarily be willing to do this. But let
them just do it. For, if they do, a Person comes in. An
Almighty Person. The Third Person of the Trinity. He is
mightier than our wills. His nature is the nature of God.

And if once we give Him honest possession, He sets to work to *change* us. He changes our wills, melts down our opposition, sets them on a new bearing, to will the will of God and to love to will it, till it becomes a consuming passion with us, till we will literally die rather than disobey God.

He changes our outlook. Having ourselves at last found a bottom to life, a heart satisfaction, a light to the mind, a way for the feet, we find ourselves joining the ranks of those who have a contribution to make to the world, not merely a merchandise to make of it. We pass from the number of the getters to the givers, and it is by the inner redirection of the Spirit that this change takes place.

Aglow ourselves with the joy of the Lord, our own needs met in Jesus, it dawns on us somehow, as on the starving lepers who found the good things in the deserted camp of the Syrians: "We do not well; this day is a day of good tidings, and we hold our peace: ... Let us go and tell..."

Moreover, a sense of responsibility comes upon us. We have been in great danger and knew it not; we were slaves and had given up hope of liberation. Now freedom, food and clothing, and a welcome home is ours. And not only ours but the world's, if they but believed it. Some know it and mock. Thousands about us do not know, through a false idea of what the good news is. Millions have yet never had a chance to hear. We are debtors. We *owe* it to our next-door neighbour as well as to the most distant of our brother men. By increasing stages a new passion inflames us. The glory of it dawns upon us. That such as we can be, not merely inheritors of eternal life, but transmitters of it. These lips can bring heaven to a hell-bound soul. We are captured by a new commission. Surely indeed we are changed.

But to carry this out means a price to be paid. In a world that shows its true nature by baring its teeth if brought into too close quarters with God, it is never an easy thing to speak of Christ. It is abnormal, fanatical. Ice has to be broken, commonplaces by-passed, the circumference of vague religious comment pierced till the centre of personal challenge is reached. Time has to be used which normally is frittered away in gossip or hobby. Concentration is necessary when it is customaiy to relax. The Spirit has begun to lead out along the way to Calvary.

Burdens grow heavier. What can be done for the souls around in business or neighbourhood, in the town and in the district where our church is located? Time must be given for prayer, for concerted action with fellow Christians. Evenings become occupied, meetings attended.

Missionary visitors give yet a wider vision. There is a world in need. How can the Gospel be taken to every creature? Can I go myself, leave home and daydreams and loved ones, risk life and health and security? To the few, the call comes plain and the great step is taken into a life set apart for all time to be lived amongst strange people, to wrestle with ignorance, disease, superstition. To the many, not that actual call comes, but a sense of a necessary share in it; money must be given, loved ones painfully yet gladly offered, and the very simplest things of everyday life become touched by the marks of the Cross—the wardrobe, the meal table, the expenditure on pleasure and luxuries—that more may be given to the spread of the kingdom. The home itself becomes more threadbare, maybe, as parlour or drawing room, once kept like a new pin for special occasions, is constantly used for "squashes" and prayer meetings.

By this way or that, the self-giving nature of God takes up its abode in our nature and produces these radical changes. They become our very nature, derived from, as C. T. Studd once wrote, "The Holy Spirit of God, one of whose chief characteristics is a pluck, a bravery, a lust for sacrifice for God, and a joy in it which crucifies all human weaknesses and natural desires of the flesh."

So let us get this clear. The evidence that the third Person of the Trinity is dwelling in me is certainly not just ecstasies and exalted feelings; it is not merely the gentler graces of love, joy, peace; it is also the sterner characteristics of God's soldier, a passion to sacrifice for a world's salvation, a courage to witness, a steadfastness in affliction, an actual doing of soldier's deeds.

We think it essential to emphasize this, for in countries where Christianity is at least the nominally accepted faith, it is easy to miss it. It was the natural accompaniment of conversion in the early church. Only "through much tribulation", they were plainly told, could they enter into the kingdom of God. The model converts of those days were born in the midst of "much affliction with joy of the Holy Ghost". The companies of believers who adhered to God's Word in its purity through the centuries ever had the marks of the martyr upon them.

In a remarkable book by E. H. Broadbent,[1] a well-documented account is given of the numerous bodies of faithful believers who have never ceased to maintain the faith from Apostolic days up to the present. Sometimes we get the idea that in the "Dark Ages", when Rome appeared to dominate the religious scene, the light had almost gone out. Not so indeed. This book shews that thousands upon thousands resisted the claims of the false church unto blood, and that the faithful followers of Christ to-day are not, as Rome would have it, schismatics from the so-called "mother church", but can trace their

[1] *The Pilgrim Church*, Pickering & Inglis, 8s.

descent in a straight line through great bodies of believing Christians who, cost what it might, never acknowledged any authority but that of the Scriptures, nor any Head of the church but Christ.

Of the early days of the Roman Empire up to A.D. 300 we all know, when "a conflict ensued in which all the resources of that mighty power were exhausted in a vain endeavour to vanquish those who never resisted or retaliated, but bore all for love of their Lord. All ther possessions were confiscated, they were imprisoned, and not only put to death in countless numbers, but every imaginable torture was added to their punishment, and every portion of the Scriptures that could be found was destroyed. Yet in the end the Roman Empire was overcome by the devotion to the Lord Jesus of those who knew Him."

But of the centuries that followed, which "unfolded the growth in worldliness and ambition of the clergy both of the Eastern and Western Catholic Churches, until they claimed entire dominion over the possessions and conscience of mankind", we realize much less what "countless saints there were who suffered all things at the hands of the dominant world-church rather than deny Christ or be turned back from following Him." The true histories of these were obliterated by their enemies as far as possible, and their writings, sharing the fate of the writers, have been destroyed. Yet movements of revival never ceased to be repeated.

In the earlier of these centuries, from A.D. 300 onwards, Asia Minor and Armenia were frequently the scene of such revivings, the churches being called Paulicians. Persecution of them reached its greatest height under the Empress Theodora, who was responsible in the ninth century for the death of about 100,000 persons; and their elders in those perilous days were asked this question before hands of consecration were laid on them: "Art thou then able to drink the cup which I am about to drink, or to be baptized with the baptism with which I am about to be baptized?" To which they answered: "I take on myself scourgings, imprisonment, tortures, reproaches, crosses, blows, tribulation and all temptations of the world which our Lord and Intercessor and the Universal and Apostolic Holy Church took upon themselves."

Likewise the Bogomils, the "Friends of God", from about A.D. 900 onward, scattered through Eastern Europe from Hungary to Bulgaria, "through their heroic stand for four centuries against overwhelming adversity must have yielded examples of faith and courage second to none in the world's history". With them were linked in common faith, practice and endurance, such better-known bodies of believers as the Albigenses in France, Waldenses in Italy, and Hussites in Bohemia.

Through the Reformation period and later, the sufferings of the churches are better known, and we only have to instance such a conference as Augsburg in 1529 which was called "The Martyr's Conference", because so many who took part in it were later put to death. Many others in those days were branded with a cross on their foreheads. In Austria the accounts of the numbers put to death and of their sufferings are terrible, yet the spread of the churches was marvellous. "There never failed to be men willing to take up the dangerous work of evangelists and elders. They went full of joy to their death. They found that God helped them to bear the cross and to overcome the bitterness of death. The fire of God burned in them."

Converts in many mission fields still have these same

experiences, especially in Moslem and Roman Catholic lands; and believers in several of the modern totalitarian states have had to choose between denial of Christ and the concentration camp.

But we Christians in our more "fortunate" circumstances do not get conditions of suffering like this forced upon us, and equally we are obviously not called upon to look for trouble and seek martyrdom, but rather to thank God that our lines are fallen in more pleasant places. But this is the point. To us also the inescapable pressure of the Spirit comes, if we are really His to the limit, which will not allow us to live our lives on the comfortable level of such a word as "God has given us richly all things to enjoy"; but rather on those others which say: "All things are lawful, but all things are not expedient"; "Though I be free from all, yet have I made myself servant to all, that I might gain the more"; "I endure all things for the elect's sake." Enjoyments there will be, many and continual, for all life has joy and zest in it when it is mediated through Christ; but a conscious binding sense of dedication will be upon us, a voluntarily accepted yoke of holy servitude. We are prisoners of the Lord, bound in spirit, even as Paul deliberately renounced certain of life's normal privileges that he might better preach the Gospel, a kind of voluntary extremism. So will we, in this way or that, according to the measure of our faith and light, gladly give up some of the lesser good to gain the greater. We shall be a people with a purpose, even as for temporal ends the athlete denies himself, the scientist devotes himself, the soldier risks himself.

In a special sense it appears that the Holy Spirit sets men apart, when they allow Him to, for special ends, and lays on them the burden that has to be borne, the price to be paid, the travail to be endured, and even the death to be died, to bring that special end about. It is what the Scripture calls God finding an intercessor. They are rare, for God in a past emergency wondered that there was no intercessor.[1] It is costly to be an intercessor, reaching far beyond the ordinary prayer-life of request and supplication, for there is expenditure of heart's blood and agony of soul in it. "He poured out His soul unto death," we read, "and was numbered with the transgressors, and bare the sin of many"; and so, it says, "He made intercession for the transgressors."

The reward of the intercessor is as great as his travail. He fulfils the law of the harvest. He goes through the processes of death, accepts them voluntarily, has them laid on him by the travailing Spirit who groans within him with groanings which cannot be uttered; and by so doing the upspringing of the harvest, resurrection life for the world, is as sure as that spring and summer follow winter.

And here he is no longer in the school of faith, but the life of faith; for this death and resurrection process is not now for his own sanctification, but for a world's need. God has at last found His servant on whom He can lay the kind of burdens the Saviour carried, not for himself and for his own growth in grace, but for others. It is a share in the fellowship of Christ's sufferings. It is the third and final meaning of the Cross in the individual life; the Cross first borne by Christ alone for our sins, then shared by us with Christ for our sanctification, and now borne in turn by us for our neighbour's salvation. It is the outworking of the Cross referred to by Paul when he said, "So death worketh in us, but life in you."

In this life of an intercessor there are positions that are gained by faith, and once gained need not be lost unless

[1] Isa. 59: 16.

we foolishly let them go. The same truth can be seen in the elementary stages of faith: once a person is saved, for instance, he knows it, glories in it, and it is in no sense hard to abide in the certainty of salvation, if the ordinary precautions for daily abiding are observed. The position of saving faith has been gained. In sanctification the same. There is the travail, the complete surrender, the battle of faith, and then the full assurance of faith. Once again a new position of faith has been reached, and the believer can abide at ease in his "Beulah land", in union and communion with his Lord, unless he deliberately forfeits his inheritance. And so in more advanced experiences, in the Christian harvest field, for which the gaining of these personal positions are but the preparation; for their real meaning has been to "teach our hands to war and our fingers to fight"; not to give us some static experience of imparted grace, but some dynamic knowledge of how to wield the weapons of faith by which God can now do through us for others what He previously did in us for ourselves. We have learned in the school of faith how to wage a good warfare on the battlefields of the Spirit, and now we can use our knowledge in the life of faith.

Christ the Intercessor, after His early years of personal training, went out to do His intercessory work at the command of the anointing Spirit, and gained His position of faith, the right to be Saviour, after three years of obedience unto death. Again and again He referred to the pressure on His spirit during those years; "I have a baptism to be baptized with, and how am I straitened until it be accomplished." To His disciples, in His early ministry, He said: "My meat is to do the will of Him that sent Me, and to finish His work." To His Father, just before Calvary: "I have finished the work Thou gavest Me to do." To the world, with His last breath: "It is finished."

It was said twice over by the writer to the Hebrews that it was through His sufferings that He was perfected as pioneer of our salvation and author of eternal life to all who obey Him.[1] And now we see Him still the Intercessor, not in the heat of battle, but enthroned in triumph. Then He was pouring out His soul unto death, but now dispensing the fruits of His victory: "able to save to the uttermost them that come unto God by Him, seeing He ever liveth to make intercession for them." On the basis of that battle once fought, that life once poured out utterly for our transgressions, He can now lead captivity captive and give the constant gift of His Holy Spirit to men.

We also, in our lesser spheres, can gain positions of faith and do the full work of an intercessor. At the roots of every golden harvest field of souls reaped by the Spirit of God there lies a life or lives which have been intercessors, lives lived under a deep and enduring sense of urgency, clear direction, absolute dedication to the task. They have *had* to carry this specific burden in prayer night and day. They have had to go and live long years amongst that strange tribe. They have had to give and give and give again out of their sometimes dwindling resources. They have had to stick to their tract distributing, open-air meetings, sick visitation, or whatever it may be, large or small; for the intensity of the devotion, not the size of the commission, is what matters to God.

And then comes a time in such a single-hearted ministry when the break occurs, sometimes in the lifetime of the intercessors, sometimes after, and it seems as if heaven's windows are open and God's storehouses un-

[1] This is the special teaching of the book of Hebrews with reference to the high priesthood of Christ. See 2: 9-18; 4: 14-16; 5: 1-10; 7: 22-28; 9: 11-15; 10: 5-14; 12: 1-3.

locked, and the blessing just flows. It is the Pentecost after Calvary. Such a truth can be seen in the lives of the great intercessors. Abraham's whole life as stranger and pilgrim, dwelling in tents with Isaac and Jacob, was such an intercession, and God's covenant to him has never failed through the centuries; Israel was always able to ask for God's intervention on the ground of His oath to Abraham. Moses paid the price for Israel's redemption, and Joshua enjoyed the success. David had the same covenant blessing for a successor on his throne. And, supremely, of course, the Saviour and the church He bought with His blood.

It is good to understand this spiritual law of the harvest. It helps us to fulfil our ministry strategically, intelligently. We see where we are going, not just faithfully but rather hopelessly witnessing a good confession in a difficult place, but understanding that if we pay the full price of our calling and realize that our labours and lonelinesses, our setbacks and disheartenments, our heart agonies and pleadings with God and man, are that price, that necessary dying process of the seed; then we shall go on and go through, and faith may flicker but will not fail. We are fulfilling certain unchangeable laws of the Spirit under the guidance and by the inspiration of the Spirit.

We believe that in many a work of God—in our own missionary society, for instance, through the price paid by our founder C. T. Studd; in the China Inland Mission, likewise, through Dr. Hudson Taylor; in the Salvation Army, through General Booth; in the Orphan Homes, through Dr. Barnardo and George Müller—we, the succeeding generations, enjoy the abundant fruits of the intercession made by these great men of God, an intercession in which we, of course, in measure are also partners; and there indeed also lies the danger of a second and third

generation work; that so much comes easily to them
which others have paid the price to obtain, and the battle
spirit, the fire, the zeal, the sacrifice of the founders dies
away.

We can never get beyond the Cross. There certainly is
a sense in which even the Cross can be given a wrongful
prominence. It is not meant to be in the foreground, but
background, of the scene; not the superstructure, but
foundation, of the building. To parade the Cross, whether
in its outward form, as do the Roman Catholics with their
crucifixes, or in its inward dynamic by over-display of,
or overemphasis on, the cost of discipleship, is to draw
wrongful attention to it. It is life, not death, that is our
message, a living and returning, not a crucified, Christ.
C. T. Studd put it rightly when he wrote on a postcard,
when leaving for the heart of Africa:

> *Take my life and let it be*
> *A* hidden *Cross revealing Thee.*

But, at the same time, just because the world lies in darkness and error, and because we Christians ourselves can
so easily be turned out of the narrow way, there has to
be constant attention called to our foundations, and constant emphasis laid upon the fact there is no other foundation to the kingdom of God than the Cross of Christ.

We know this very well as our entry into life. We have
learned it as our way of deliverance from inner bondage.
We see it now and finally as the law of harvest. We never
get beyond the Cross, either in time or eternity, for we
have learned that release of life and power on the spiritual
level can only come about through death on the natural
level. "Self-control", which is the Cross in action, "re-
leases energy on a new level." This remains true in the
tiniest as in the biggest things of life, and it takes us back

to the essential message of this book, and, much more important, of The Book. Grasp it and one has grasped "the secret of the Lord". That "way" is, to repeat once more, that every battle of life concerning ourselves, our circumstances, or our neighbours, is first fought and won *within*. The battleground is ourselves, and the victory is Christ's Cross in its inner operation. If we turn our attention away from *our* reactions, resentments, proposed activities, with reference to a situation, and die to them, die till we are inwardly free from the motions of self, then God's voice can be heard, His way seen and His outlook accepted; and then we can receive, believe and act on it. Resurrection life has begun within ourselves, and will forthwith express itself through look and word and deed. What is won within is won without, what is lost within is lost without, and the secret is the Cross.

Paul wrote a triumphant letter on the secret of the Cross applied to daily life, in his second epistle to the Corinthians. It glows with glory.[1] It rings with triumph.[2] Yet almost every chapter has reference to the intensity of his sufferings, his endless trials, his "fightings without and fears within". Paul is seen in his human weakness in that letter, and he describes right through, from first chapter to last, how he learned by experience the great secret. Almost his first words were that he had the sentence of death in himself that he should not trust in himself but in God who raises the dead; in the middle he has a whole passage on bearing about in his body the dying of the Lord Jesus, that the life also of Jesus might be made manifest in his body; and at the end he tells how he gloried in the revelation that when he was weak then was he strong; gloried to the point that in future he would actually take pleasure in anything which weakened or frustrated or brought to

[1] See Chapters 3 and 4. [2] 2: 14.

nothing his life on the natural level. It was a well-learned lesson, for he was able to say, in this same letter, that though he walked in the flesh (felt all the limitations of an ordinary man), yet he warred not after the flesh; the weapons of his warfare were not fleshly, but mighty through God. He had learned how to live by dying, how to fight by yielding; and he summed it all up by saying that he knew and desired to know no other way than his Master's, who "though He was crucified through weakness, yet liveth by the power of God"; adding that "we also are weak, sharing His weakness, but with Him we shall be full of life to deal with (this or that thing) through the power of God."

APPENDIX

THE DIALECTIC OF LIFE AND ITS ORIGIN

To some minds, origins are of little interest; facts are facts and let them be faced as such. To others an attempt at the explanation of the origin of things can alone satisfy the heart and mind. They must not only know what a thing does, but why and how it does it. And in the things of the Spirit my own mind was not set at rest until, greatly helped by some of the mighty seers and expositors of the ages, and always endeavouring to keep within the confines of God's Word, some satisfying conception of origins was arrived at. It may well be controversial to some, difficult or unnecessary to others, even presumptuous to yet others, searching beyond where we need to search into the nature of "the eternal, immortal, invisible"; but is has helped me, and so, writing I trust in a spirit of reverence, I pass on this brief outline in the form of an appendix.[1]

The problem which immediately meets us at all times is the right understanding and handling of the opposing forces in our daily life; for it is obvious at every turn and corner alike, in things large and small, that we are faced with that which pulls in a wrong direction, stirs in us wrong feelings, frustrates, depresses, raises impossible barriers. The answer to such questions as how these things come to be, how they affect us as they do, what their uses are, and what are to be our reactions, gives us the absolutely necessary key to a continuous mastery over

[1] This is an extract from a longer pamphlet, a few copies of which have been duplicated for private circulation and can be obtained, if still in stock, from the author.

them; or, rather, to the proper and creative redirection of them; indeed, to making us see enemies as friends; for when all things and people, even oppositions and opposers, can be seen in a friendly light, the secret is ours.[1]

We must start at the beginning, although it may seem a long way back. We must start with the elemental power of choice, which is stimulated to action by the constant necessity of choosing between alternatives; then the fatefulness of choice, and the final fixation of choice in character and destiny. For here is the very substructure of life.

We find on analysis that the fundamental instinct of all life is desire, attraction to itself. In nature, the forces of gravity shew this; in physics, the unceasing attraction of the positive and negative particles of electricity, the protons and electrons which form the atom; or, at the other end of the scale, the power which maintains the solar system in equilibrium; all these have no different origin from the basic, all-governing instincts of self-preservation, acquisition, achievement, propagation in man. All is desire. Desire is the primal energy of life. Desire in its perfected form of love is the foundation of God's nature: "Thou hast created all things, and for Thy pleasure they are and were created"; "the mystery of His will, according to His good pleasure which He purposed in Himself."

Examine desire further and we learn this. Attraction, by its activity, brings into being its opposite, repulsion. Thus if I draw something towards me, although the nature of my desire is to attract, grasp, hold—a tightening, a hardening, immobilizing quality; yet the very fact of my drawing brings its opposite into activity, motion. Attraction causes a thing to move. But mobility is the opposite to the tightening, hardening, grasping of attraction: the nature of mobility is to go out from itself in outflow,

[1] 2 Cor. 12: 10.

output. Thus desire is seen to have a dual manifestation: at its heart is a conflict of equal but opposing forces, whose tension is the root of all manifested life. This is seen in the fact that all life is the contrast, tension and interaction of opposites; thesis and antithesis which make the working synthesis: male and female, light and darkness, spirit and matter, and so on endlessly. Nothing shows this more clearly than the twentieth-century discovery of the composition of the atom, once thought to be like a minute and indestructible billiard ball, now known to consist of various numbers of electrons, negative particles of electricity, revolving at immense speed around a nucleus consisting of positive particles, protons. The quality of tension causes the rotation. The proton, the positive, attracts towards itself; the electron, the negative, attracts towards itself in the opposite direction: the tension between the two, being of equal force, resulting in the rotation of the one around the other. Such is the vast power of their attraction that particles knocked by collision out of the atom are known to travel at 45,000,000 miles an hour![1] The one phenomenon of attraction, repulsion and rotation is shown to be the structure of all visible things; every particle of matter, every chemical substance. And, in the spiritual realm, these same threefold qualities form the nature of self-hood, the structure of desire: to grasp, and its opposite, to give; to draw to oneself, and its opposite, to go out to others; and the tension and interaction between these opposites form what James calls, in a significant phrase, the whirling "wheel of nature",[2] the activity of all intelligent life. Now, it is at this point in self-conscious beings that choice takes the dominant position. Man stands in between these warring opposites of "get" and "give". Shall it be a constant raging, whirling

[1] Alpha particles.   [2] James 3: 6 (margin).

struggle, first one in control and then the other? That is fallen nature with its endless restlessness and unsatisfied hunger. Or shall it be the yielding of the "get" instinct to the "give"? That is the nature of God reinstated in man by the Cross and the Spirit. For by that means the "get" nature is harmonized with the "give" nature, finding its pleasure (its "get"-instinct satisfied) in giving. That is the synthesis of the eternal nature. That is the Kingdom of heaven.

But it ought to be noted that this separation in the self, these warring opposites of our nature, which can only be reconciled in Christ, were never meant to be known by us in conflict. In God, the Three-in-One, they have been unified from all eternity and are only seen in the glories and graces of the Father, Son and Holy Spirit.

But we must remember that what is a derived selfhood in man and a created condition in matter has its origin in God. The idea that the world was created out of nothing is a myth exploded by the Bible itself. Thus it says of matter that "the visible was made out of the invisible";[1] and of man that God created man in his own image and breathed His own breath into Him. The truth is that, each in their own measure, all creation has only one life in it, the life of God. All creatures are but God's love compacted into material form. That driving-wheel of desire seen in man and matter is first of all the foundation of God's own Being.

God is the Self from which all selves have come. All the tremendous forces that have created and conserved this universe issue from that one Self, the first quality of whose nature is this self-same desire. But God is not mere desire. His is sublimated, disciplined, desire. He is love. In Him, desire always has been but the raw material of

[1] Heb. 11: 3 (Moffatt).

love. The whirling wheel of self-hood has from everlasting been the hidden fuel; the driving force of the light and love and eternal self-giving of the Father of lights with whom is no variableness, neither shadow of turning.

We must speak as a man. We must divide the indivisible, describe the Infinite in finite terms in order to make the truth plain to our finite minds. We have already pointed to a basic self-nature in the Holy One which, as a fact, has never in a separate sense been manifest in Him. Only in the disruptive experience of man have this whirling wheel of anguish, these contrary forces, this naked self-hood, come to be known and felt; and, only to help man understand and readjust his chaotic nature, do we trace this self back to its source in God. In doing so we take apart what never has been apart in Him, till Lucifer made the severance. For, in the Eternal Being, those elemental forces of His nature are eternally centred, integrated and yielded up to the love of the Son, the second Person of the Godhead, who has eternally dwelt in the bosom of the Father. We say again, we are dividing the indivisible; but to explain it in human language we would say it is as if the Father represents the eternal desire principle, the self-hood; the begetting of the Son is, as it were, the moment when the Father "chooses" to pour all the energies of His Being out from Himself into the love of another, thus begetting what we know as the kingdom of heaven, as love, service, selflessness, meekness, goodness, grace. It is as if we see a Cross in the very heart of eternity, when the Eternal One "dies" to Himself and "lives" to His Son. As if, at that moment, a self which could potentially become a kingdom of darkness and self-seeking, became eternally immersed, sublimated, resurrected into a realm of light and love, an eternal will to all goodness, centred around His Son. Such is a mere human figure of speech, for in reality Father and Son have been co-existent from everlasting, one in the other; there has been no moment of choice or moment of begetting, no dying to "self" and rising to "others", but rather an eternal, indivisible unity of being, Father and Son together in their eternal embrace revealing an eternal nature of love; and from them proceeding the Spirit, their Spirit, Father and Son proceeding forth in action, as framer and artificer of all the glories and marvels of the universe; the love which has its source in the Father-Son relationship, but which, to fulfil its love nature, must overflow and outflow as Spirit in endless forms of self-expression, all created of love and by love to participate in the endless blessings of the happy Trinity.

An earthly symbol of the Three-in-One is fire, light and life. Fire, as seen in the sun, is the source of all life on this planet. By itself it is a terrible and consuming power. Infringe the laws of nature and approach too close to it, and pain and destruction are the penalty. Yet from this flaming source radiate all the marvels and beauties, colours and warmth of the meek and gentle light. No fire means no light. No light means no life on earth, for the light passes into all nature, quickens, sustains, gives colour and form to all things. To perform its life-giving function on the earth this trinity-in-unity must be in operation: the fire must burn, the light must shine, life must be quickened in plant and animal.

But to earth dwellers the sun is never meant to be known and felt except by its blessings of light and warmth. The fire, as it were, is only known and mediated to us in its eternal begetting of the light. We recognize that flaming centre, we realize that it is the burning source of the light, but we know our rightful relationship to it; we gratefully bask in its blessings, but we keep our proper

distance. The laws of fire and light and their effect on the
human body are fixed and we wisely obey them.

So it was meant to be when the Three-in-One first made
created beings. They were to share in the kingdom of love
by giving themselves to God; as Father is given to Son,
and Son to Father, and Spirit to both. But first they must
be selves, real selves, conscious of self-hood, conscious
of those elemental forces inherent in their nature, derived
by creation from the Father-self. Choice must be the de-
ciding factor. As God, if we may so say, "chose" the way
of love, the way of His eternal nature, so must His sons
become fixed in the way of His Spirit by persistent choice.
Desire, will, imagination, ambition, must be at work, the
whirling wheel of nature.

Immediately then, there confronts them a fundamental
selection of one of two ways, symbolized for Adam and
Eve in a later creation by the tree of knowledge of good
and evil, and the tree of life. By setting the will to the
former, self chooses itself; the way of the kingdom of
heaven by which all selves find full expression and satisfaction in the give and take of loving service, the Father-
Son-Spirit way, is spurned in its garments of meekness
and humility; the glorious plan of the ages by which each
self, each creature, is a happy vital unit in a vast organic
whole, each a member of one universal body, a chord in
the harmony of heaven, is shattered: and the self makes the
dreadful plunge back into itself; it shall be "I will", not
"God wills"; the drive of its own desires shall be its only
master; it shall be its own god; its own great powers of
mind and will and passion shall carve out its own destiny.
Thus the circuit is snapped which joins it in bonds of love
and unity with all creatures and the Creator. Two kingdoms have come into being, where there was only one.
The kingdom of self, created to be only the hidden food

and fuel of the kingdom of love, has made its separate appearance.

An unknown monstrosity, named evil, has appeared on the stage. As a separate entity it had no original existence. At the dawn of creation, when the morning stars sang together, no such element was named or known. For it is a usurper, a thief. Our examination of it proves it to be misused, misapplied, good. That hidden self, having chosen to cut itself off from its source and its sphere of co-operative service, has come into the open as an independent, rival and antagonistic way of life. It will seek its own ends. It will satisfy its own lusts. It has powers of its own and will use them. It will be "free". It has formed a kingdom, a rebel realm. It is evil.

But is it free? Look again at this kingdom of self. It is "the back parts" of God. It is the underlying forces which vitalize His love, joy and peace. It is the fire which begets the light. These same forces, this same fire has passed from the Father into His offspring, and formed their separate and free selves; yet, though separate and distinct personalities, we are still, so far as our basic nature is concerned, in Him and part of Him: "In Him we live and move and have our being." Our selves still remain part of His one Self, and derive their natural life from Him. But in turning away from our natural destiny, we perform an unnatural act; we break the laws of eternal nature and we meet with the consequences of all broken law. Fire begets light. Infringe the laws of fire, plunge your hands into the blaze, the hot and fierce source of its blessings, and you receive not warmth and light, but burns and scars; blessings become cursings; gentleness, wrath.

Thus it is that the hidden kingdom of self-hood, the root and raw material of the kingdom of heaven, becomes the kingdom of darkness; all evil passions flourish in it,

all discord and disease, all hatred, lust and cruelty. It is
the kingdom of Lucifer and his fallen hosts. It is fore-
shadowing of that lake which burneth with fire for ever
and ever. These know God, not as "the meek and gentle
light of heaven", but in His hidden fire-root into which
they have unlawfully penetrated. They have plunged their
hands in the fire, instead of basking in the light. To the
froward He shows Himself froward. And here we find
the true explanation of hell.

How often has the question disturbed thinking Christians. How can there be a hell? How can a God of love
condemn men to a lake of fire? How reconcile wrath and
mercy in the Father of our Lord Jesus Christ? The answer
is here given. The avenging fires of hell are a part of
God, an inevitable part of His nature, for they are the
very same fires which flame up in love in the heavenly
kingdom. Never would they have been known or felt as
fierce and hellish fires, had not Lucifer and his hosts, and
then man through Lucifer's deception, turned back from
God's light-kingdom to His fire-kingdom. Natures that
were made to live in union with the Father of lights in the
beauties and blessings of the heavenlies had now chosen
of their own free will to extinguish the light and plunge
unlawfully into the dark fiery energies of the independent
self-hood, only to find themselves in the resistless grip of
their tormenting pride and wrath and passion, consumed
of their own lusts yet never satisfied, in the unassuaged
burnings of the whirling wheel of conflicting desire. Yet
these very tumults and ragings are still the movings of
God in them, not God in mercy but God in wrath. All
nature, whether of angels, devils (fallen angels), or men,
is but a flame from the central fire and remains eternally
fed from its burning source; but, to the merciful, He shows
Himself merciful in the gentle fire of love; by the froward

He is found to be froward, a consuming fire of wrath that burns in the pride and malice and rage of that distorted self-hood. Such is hell. As much a part of the inevitable nature of things as heaven; for hell and heaven are really the two sides of the one eternal element, the consuming life-fire which is God's nature, burning in love or burning in wrath, just according to which we immerse ourselves in.

God does not *make* hell. God only made heaven and all things to have the nature of heaven. Lucifer and his rebel followers, by breaking themselves off from the heavenly meekness and love, discovered for themselves the hidden and unknown fire-source of heaven's light, the burning wheel of the elemental self-nature of God. This now became their kingdom, their hell-fire, both in themselves and in their sphere of activity, the earth which they corrupted. A God of wrath and judgment, rage and fury, is all that they can know, a God of vengeance, of tempest, of destruction.

Hell has become now, not first a place, but a condition. Wherever the rebel-self dominates, there is hell; there are the burnings of God's wrath. Within, where the fires of anger, hate, malice, lust, rage in the soul, there is hell; without, where war, rapine, disease and death stalk abroad, there also is hell. All is still God's kingdom, all are still God's children; but it is the kingdom of God's anger, the children of God's wrath.

With the wrath, on our earth, is mingled mercy, for this is still the day of probation and salvation. Two kingdoms strive within us and around, the realms of darkness and light. All things are compounded of mingled good and evil: if there are thorns, there are also flowers; if there is night, there is also day; if there are poisons, there are also health-giving foods. But the night cometh, the ever-

lasting darkness in which the apostate angels already
dwell, where no tokens of mercy mingle with the fruits
of wrath, as on this earth; no sun, no flowers and fruits,
no friendly and beautiful creatures: only the anguishing
wheel of apostate, insatiable self-hood, the rage, the selfishness, the unassuaged passions of men and angels
whose characters have become fixed as devils.

Such is hell in its final form; the eternal home carved
out in the outer darkness by the free will of free beings,
who preferred the kingdom of self to the kingdom of God,
and persisted in their choice. It is God's hell? Yes, for all
is God's. Is such a hell God's plan and will and making?
A thousand times no. It is the rebel will of His creatures
that brought hell into existence. It is the unlawful penetration into the realm of forces in God and His creatures
which only exist for universal blessing, and the perversion
of these forces to selfish ends: the consequence being
harmony transformed into disharmony; peace into war;
love into hate; joy into pain; the very ingredients of the
hellish state.